MORE PRAISE FOR
The Secrets of Happily Married Women

"Every woman can benefit through understanding how to bring out the best in a man. Scott Haltzman and Theresa Foy DiGeronimo brilliantly reveal this secret."

John Gray, author, *Men Are from Mars, Women Are from Venus*

"Finally. The first book that men will want women to read! Scott Haltzman has created a practical gem that allows women to focus on learning how to receive love from their husband. He advocates the Platinum (not Golden) Rule and urges women to 'Do Unto Your Husband What He Wants Done Unto Him,' so they can find the marital happiness they long for."

Jon Carlson, distinguished professor, Governors State University, and author, *Time for a Better Marriage*

"This groundbreaking book combines a pro-female, pro-male, and pro-marriage approach to life and couple satisfaction. It's very user-friendly, with shared secrets and research gems coupled with a large dose of humor that makes clinical points personally relevant and easy to relate to. The sex self-test in Chapter Five is an effective tool to help set realistic expectations. This will be a particularly helpful book for couples to increase understanding, acceptance, and value in their lives and marriage."

Barry McCarthy, professor of psychology, American University, and author, *Rekindling Desire* and *Getting It Right This Time*

"Scott Haltzman has made the deep secrets of happy marriage accessible, memorable, and inspiring. He writes with a light touch that makes the reading thoroughly enjoyable. Don't miss this engaging book!"

Susan Page, author, *Why Talking Is Not Enough: 8 Loving Actions That Will Transform Your Marriage* and *If I'm So Wonderful, Why Am I Still Single?*

"This book delivers! *The Secrets of Happily Married Women* is jam-packed with research, ancient truths, street-smart wisdom, and years of advice from the psychiatrist's couch. Page after page provides a sensitive, sensible guide to a satisfying relationship. Buy it, read it, reap the benefits. I'm going to."

> Patricia Love, certified love educator and coauthor, *How to Improve Your Marriage Without Talking About It*

"Dr. Haltzman uses clear and practical language to show women how to engage and support their husbands in their efforts to please them. He shares the 'secrets' women really need to know about men, so this book is a 'must-read'! Reading this book should start your list of New Year's resolutions."

> Susan L. Blumberg, Ph.D., coauthor, *Fighting for Your Marriage* and *12 Hours to a Great Marriage*

"Wives, what we've all been longing for has finally arrived. . . . This masterpiece eliminates the womanly guesswork and illuminates the path to true marital happiness with honest, sincere, frank . . . (and even humorous) information."

> Sheryl P. Kurland, relationship/marriage trainer and author, *Everlasting Matrimony: Pearls of Wisdom from Couples Married 50 Years or More*

The Secrets of Happily Married Women

How to Get More Out of Your Relationship by Doing Less

Scott Haltzman, M.D., and
Theresa Foy DiGeronimo

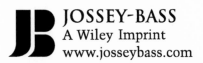

JOSSEY-BASS
A Wiley Imprint
www.josseybass.com

Published by Jossey-Bass
A Wiley Imprint
989 Market Street, San Francisco, CA 94103-1741—www.josseybass.com

The anecdotes in this book are based on the life experience of the authors and the clinical work and research of Dr. Haltzman. To protect confidentiality, names and identifying characteristics of clients have been changed, or represent composite identities of clients.

Readers should be aware that Internet Web sites offered as citations and/or sources for further information may have changed or disappeared between the time this was written and when it is read.

Jossey-Bass books and products are available through most bookstores. To contact Jossey-Bass directly call our Customer Care Department within the U.S. at 800-956-7739, outside the U.S. at 317-572-3986, or fax 317-572-4002.

Jossey-Bass also publishes its books in a variety of electronic formats. Some content that appears in print may not be available in electronic books.

Library of Congress Cataloging-in-Publication Data
Haltzman, Scott, date.
  The secrets of happily married women : how to get more out of your relationship by doing less / Scott Haltzman, and Theresa Foy DiGeronimo.
      p. cm.
  Includes bibliographical references.
  ISBN 978-0-7879-9612-3 (cloth)
  ISBN 978-0-470-40180-4 (paper)
  1. Wives. 2. Marriage—Handbooks, manuals, etc. I. DiGeronimo, Theresa Foy. II. Title.
  HQ759.H189 2008
  646.7'8—dc22   2007035655

Printed in the United States of America
FIRST EDITION
PB Printing   10 9 8 7 6 5 4 3 2 1

Contents

Acknowledgments   vii

Introduction   1

1. Know Your Husband   7

2. Nurture His Needs—and Yours   45

3. Fight Better   63

4. Talk Less   103

5. Have Lots of Sex   127

6. Take Charge of Your Own Happiness   163

7. Heal Thyself   191

Epilogue: When Mamma's Happy, Everybody's Happy   209

Notes   211

About the Authors   215

To my wife, Susan, who has helped me be a better man.
Scott Haltzman

To my husband, Mick, who has given me a
quarter century of happiness.
Theresa Foy DiGeronimo

Acknowledgments

When my editor, Alan Rinzler, agreed to publish *The Secrets of Happily Married Women*, he spoke with Theresa and me about giving my wife, Susan, an opportunity to coauthor the book. Susan didn't have to think long before declining the offer. By making such a decision, she taught me my first secret of happy wives: when your fanatical, obsessive, and perfectionistic husband invites you to write a book with him, say no!

Yet I think that while declining the invitation to help write this book, Susan knew I could not have succeeded without her support, love, and encouragement. "Thanks" doesn't say enough, Susan, and no words ever will express my genuine appreciation.

Special thanks, also, to my children, Matthew and Alena, for inspiring me and standing by me while I toiled.

Alan Rinzler deserves my appreciation for his vision and clarity. Theresa Foy DiGeronimo for her writing skills and her unflappable positive spirit. I know now why her husband is in awe of her—she's amazing.

Thank you to my agent, Lydia Wills of Paradigm. I am also thankful to Lori Ames at Wesman Public Relations in New

York, Newberry Public Relations in Providence, Rhode Island, Tracy Williams of TradeWinds Communications in Denver, and Growing Minds Website Designs for helping me get the word out about the work I do.

There are many individuals in the marriage movement who have helped me along the way, and I am thankful to all of them. Leading the pack, however, is Diane Sollee of Smart-Marriages.com; I am indebted to her for believing in me and encouraging me.

Finally, I thank all the women and men whose stories make up the content of this book. I had reached out to patients, friends, coworkers, and a large Internet community, and asked people to teach me how to make marriages great. They've shared their secrets with me so that I can share them with you. When you're done reading this book, I hope you'll share them with others; when you do, I'll add you to the list of people to whom I'm grateful!

—Scott Haltzman

Thank you to my coauthor, Scott Haltzman. I am lucky to have had the opportunity to work with such a fine man who was always willing to consider another point of view and who was open to working a chapter over and over until it was finally just right.

I also thank our editor, Alan Rinzler, whose vision has driven this book from the very beginning, and I want to note the valuable assistance of everyone at Wiley/Jossey-Bass who has helped this project reach its final stage, including Carol Hartland, Muna Farhat, Seth Schwartz, Susan Geraghty, and Jennifer Wenzel.

—Theresa Foy DiGeronimo

Introduction

In my twenty years as a practicing psychiatrist, I have worked with many women who sometimes question whether they are able to get through the day. I expect that. After all, people seek me out because something's not altogether right in their lives.

Yet in my medical practice and in my personal life, I meet women from time to time who seem to fit a different profile. They have stress in their lives, sure. They have bosses who are jerks, and their husbands are not clones of a chick-flick Hollywood hero. Yet despite falling short of enjoying storybook lives, these women still have a spark about them, an air of confidence, and a sense of somehow being able to keep their head while surrounded by all the chaos that circulates around them.

The most exciting thing about these women is that almost without exception, they are very happy with their marriages. As a marriage therapist, I have been eager to learn more about these women. Who are they, and why do they seem so together? As a scientist, I researched. I started talking to happily married women in my psychiatric practice. I examined medical and psychological textbooks and Internet sites. In late 2006, I launched an Internet site called HappilyMarriedWomen.com. On this site, I surveyed women to learn more about the approaches to marriage—the beliefs they had, the ways they interacted with their husbands—that lead to feelings of contentment.

I had some experience with using the World Wide Web to research these issues. In 2006, my coauthor Theresa and I published *The Secrets of Happily Married Men: Eight Ways to Win Your Wife's Heart Forever*, which was based on contributions from over a thousand individuals who had found my site and shared their insights. One of the findings that emerged from the "Married Men" phase of my research was that women and men take radically different approaches to making their marriage a success. Men tend to talk about strategy; planning; step 1, step 2, and (brace yourself for a real shock here) step 3. On the basis of the message men gave me, I presented my thesis, which formed the basis for my book: Men, make marriage your job.

I told men that if they treated their marriages with the same sense of purpose, resolve, and single-minded devotion that they have applied in the workplace, they'd have happy wives and, by extension, happy marriages. The message resonated with husbands everywhere, who informed me that I had helped their marriages. It was like music to my ears.

But my ears also picked up another sound. It came from women, and it wasn't exactly music. Women also heard my message, and they loved that I was helping men do better at marriage. But when it came to my main message, many women disagreed. Take my interview with Robin Roberts on *Good Morning America*.

As I explained how I use my work skills to succeed at marriage, she reflected back, "You say, 'apply the same principle to success in the job at home,' but, you know, won't some guys say, 'Look, I work forty hours a week; why should I make my marriage a job as well?'" I answered the question, but it gave me pause to think. Then I realized why the exchange stuck with me: almost every woman (and not a single man that I can recall) who interviewed me about the book raised the same concern: "Who needs more work?"

It became clear to me that women weren't just asking a question; they were making a statement. Today's woman has taken on the roles of full-time employee, social coordinator, child advocate, caregiver for parents, homemaker, and sexual partner, while simultaneously trying to tend to her personal needs, such as working out, dieting, studying, or meditating. Moreover, women have taken on the role of processing, interpreting, and integrating all the emotional goings-on in the life of her husband. So when I talk about treating marriage like work, it's no wonder women balk! Throughout America, I heard the hue and cry: women work hard enough! Don't give us more work!

Eventually I caught on, and realized that *The Secrets of Happily Married Men* works fine for men (better than fine!), but it just won't do for women. Women's secrets differ from men's, and it was the women who taught me that. As I listened to the women who found happiness in their marital bonds, I realized that although they had as many day-to-day obligations as other women, they didn't view their marriage as "work." Rather than view their marriage as another task to accomplish, they looked to the connection with their husbands as a source of strength and as a refuge from the stresses of everyday life. And, unlike husbands in troubled marriages, these guys didn't shy away from the emotional closeness that their wives sought. They were right there by their sides, in high spirits because their wives were happy. They all wanted to please their wives by being better men and better husbands (and—because men are in fact different from women—were willing to "work on it" without adding any work for their wives).

Happily married women are the ones who know how, seemingly effortlessly, to shape the kind of loving relationship they desire. They have mastered the magic of touching a man so deeply that he wants to be more—he wants to be better. And you too have the raw material to do the same for your marriage.

You, like most Americans, chose the person with whom you wanted to spend your life. You sought him out because he had character qualities that you liked, he turned you on, he shared values with you, and he wanted many of the same things out of life that you wanted. You and he decided together that you would share a life, and together you stood on the altar and exchanged rings, till death do you part.

Besides the man your husband is, the love that bound you together, and the pledge that you shared on your wedding day, you have one more quality at your disposal to ensure that you can find the kind of marriage you seek: you're a woman. Without exception, happily married women recognize that their female traits are indeed a source of strength and influence within the marriage, and they use their womanhood to get the most out of their relationship with their husbands. Studies have shown that women have different brains than men, and these brains are acted on by a different array of hormones. Females have a more attuned sense of emotional connectedness; they are better able to express their feelings and have radar highly sensitive to problems in the marriage. Women have a wonderful capacity to nurture, support, and bolster others, not to the exclusion of getting their own needs met, but in a collaborative way that draws out the best qualities in husband, wife, and children.

The relationship that you've been seeking is all there, and (as the Good Witch of the North tells Dorothy) it's been there all along. *The Secrets of Happily Married Women* will show you the ways that other women have inspired their husbands to be partners in a truly happy marriage, and help create a stronger and more loving and lasting connection with your husband. You deserve it!

1

Know Your Husband

When Rosa and Lucas stepped into my office for our last session, it was obvious that this was one happy couple. There's something in the way that happily married people look at each other and treat each other. They don't wear signs announcing their state of bliss, but still, everyone knows.

But it hadn't started out that way for Rosa and Lucas. At our first meeting, after routine hellos, Rosa began to explain why they had come.

She told me that she had met Lucas during a code blue at a New York City hospital. At the time, she had been a nurse there for three years, and he was a new surgical intern. She had recently ended a previous marriage, so was wary when this mild-mannered doctor struck up a conversation with her and eventually asked her out.

In the early days of their romantic relationship, Lucas was sensitive, warm, and very attentive and loving. This was the kind of man Rosa had been looking for.

"I wanted to know everything about him," she said, "what made him tick, what made him afraid, what made him happy."

Rosa thought she had all the answers by the time they cele-
brated their wedding day. But, a few months later, she began
to get frustrated that Lucas seemed to be more devoted to the
hospital than to her. Finally, they ended up having a heated
argument over what Rosa called his obsessive dedication to his
work, his self-absorption, and his cruel negligence of his wife.

When she finished berating him, she was shocked at the
words he threw back at her: "You knew who I was when you
married me. Now you want me to change. This is who I am.
Why can't you accept that?" How could he make such a hurtful comment and still claim to love her?

"If he really loves me," she said looking at him rather than
me, "he'd stop working so much and spend more time with me.
Right?"

From Rosa's point of view, the answer was an obvious yes.
Either Lucas signs on to work fewer hours or the marriage is
over. Rosa was hanging on to an either-or view of how husbands should behave; at that point, she was not a good example of a happily married woman

So when she came to my office hoping I could save her marriage by making Lucas change, my first step was to introduce
her to Secret 1: Know Your Husband. Understand his true
nature—and then use that information to your advantage.

THE CORE NATURE OF MEN

By getting to know a man's inborn traits, a woman can enjoy
his strengths as well as better understand his weaknesses. At
the same time, this knowledge puts her in a position where
she can use her mysterious yet wonderful feminine nature to
bring out the best in this man she loves.

Of course, in some cases there are things that a man has to agree to change or the marriage may not be able to be saved. If he's shooting heroin, blowing money on scratch tickets, going to strip clubs, or using violence in the household, then the Popeye motto, "I yam who I yam," just doesn't cut it. But in most other cases, any marriage will be a happier one if the husband and wife capitalize on the things that make them "who I am" and make them both feel whole and proud (and focus less on the things that do not!).

In this chapter, we'll take a close look at the nature of a typical male, a nature honed through millennia of biological and societal conditioning, and explore ways that you can both enjoy who he is and gently persuade him to be even better.

Who Is This Guy?

With that goal in mind, you can (as Rosa did) begin to ask yourself, "Who is this guy?" "What makes him tick?" "Why does he act the way he does?" In the answers, you may find that your husband has some funny, weird, annoying, and idiosyncratic ways of doing things that are quite different from the way you do things—not necessarily "wrong," just uniquely his.

As soon as Rosa learned to better read Lucas's male nature, she was able to give *less* time and emotional energy to the impossible task of making her man change because *she* wanted him to, and to put more emphasis on getting *him* to want to change. It wasn't long before Lucas chose to drop those excessive overtime hours and run home to his new wife, now a very happily married woman. How did she get him to do that? Well, that's the secret I'm ready to share.

Secret 1 will explore seven of the many reasons why men see the world differently than women, and how knowing those differences gives women the remarkable opportunity to get exactly what they want and need out of their marriages:

1. Men need to feel cared for.
2. Men need acknowledgment of their efforts.
3. Men have trouble verbalizing love and regret.
4. Men need to protect their families.
5. Men need to be right and in control.
6. Men need action.
7. Men have an undeniably strong attraction to females.

When I think about the uncanny ability of a good woman to change a man's tendency to have a self-centered, ego-driven nature, I'm reminded of that scene in the movie *As Good as It Gets* when Jack Nicholson's character says to Helen Hunt's character, "You make me want to be a better man." It is her reply that explains why it's worth the effort to teach men how to be more than they think they can be. She says simply, "That's maybe the best compliment of my life."

There. That is the magic power women have: to touch a man so deeply by caring for him that he wants to be more and better. At their core, men are hardwired to want to please their mate and make them happy. Understanding your man's nature will help you touch the core of who he is and get back from him all that you need to be happily married.

Consider the following, not as rules, but as guidelines that might differentiate you from your husband and give you insight into the many ways you can use a man's nature to strengthen your marriage.

Of course, many women have these same drives. And, naturally, all these needs are not equally strong in all men. But the

REMEMBER THIS
It Starts in the Brain

Any discussion of human behavior has to include the main engine behind all thoughts and actions: the brain.

So when I talk about the brain, please remember that I am talking in broad generalizations; just as every person is different, every brain is different. To begin: There are two lobes of the brain. In most individuals, even left-handers, the left brain controls the understanding and speaking of words, the fine details of images and words, logic, mathematical sequencing, and orderliness.

The right side of the brain has a different area of specialization. Rather than appreciate the exact semantics of speech, or see the fine details of items, the right side of the brain is more big picture and holistic. The brain's centers for creativity and emotional interpretation are found in the cortex of the right brain. Music and creative movement are generated from the right side of the brain.

As a fetus's brain develops in a mother's uterus, it will begin to shape itself based on whether the growing child is a boy or a girl. Although the expression of gender traits varies from one person to the next, the hormones androgen and estrogen act on the brain to produce "typical male" or "typical female" brain types. These differences include the following:

- The male brain is 10 percent larger in mass than the female brain. (Men's heads and bodies are also larger.) Much of this larger brain consists of white matter, which shields the brain cells from trauma and keeps information running quickly along the whole cell.

- The female brain contains more gray matter than the male brain, and these gray-matter cells tend to have more connections between them. Due to these additional connectors, the cells in the female brain are more likely to interact with many other cells simultaneously.

- The visual-spatial region of the right cerebral cortex is thicker in males in the area associated with interpreting sensory data, such as measuring, doing mechanical design, perceiving direction, map reading, and working with blocks or other objects (like the car engine). In females, there are more nerve cells in the left half of the brain where language is processed.

- The brain's two distinct hemispheres are connected by a group of fibers called the corpus callosum. In women, parts of the corpus callosum are larger than they are in men. These more fully developed pathways between the two brain hemispheres may help women to better integrate information from the logical (left) brain with the intuitive (right) brain.

As you read the rest of this book, keep these differences in mind. Differences in brain structure are microscopic, but they can sometimes result in monumental differences in behavior.

goal is to avoid marital disappointment, frustration, tension, and even divorce by accepting the fact that men and women have different physical and psychological strengths and weaknesses. This understanding can be used to support the two opposing pillars needed to give a marriage a strong structure on which to build.

So read on, and get a snapshot of who your man really is. With that understanding, you too will soon be doing less work and getting more love.

MEN NEED TO FEEL CARED FOR

Men need to feel cared for? Oh no, you and your man may say. A man wants to be the one who cares for his family. He is not the weak partner who needs someone to care for him! Well, yes and no. Yes, men do want to pamper their wives and be in charge of things (as I'll explain later in this chapter), but there's no denying that many of them also have a strong need to be cared for by their wives. If men didn't want to be taken care of, we would not be so accustomed to hearing women say, "He's such a baby when he gets sick" and "He acts like he thinks I'm his mother and will indulge all his needs" and "Sometimes I feel like my husband is my third (or fourth, or fifth) child." Sound familiar? Most men do have distinct moments when they express dependency on a mother figure and a desire to be taken care of. This is common and natural among men.

I confess to having this need myself at times. On Tuesday nights I work late, usually until after 8:00 P.M. Because I don't get a chance to eat dinner until I come home, I hold on to the secret hope that when I arrive at the end of that long day, my wife will have some leftovers heated up for me. More often than not, Tuesday is pizza-delivery night in my house. When Susan thinks to warm up the oven and put a few slices in before I get home, it makes me feel taken care of. I'm not talking about an intellectualized process; it's an instinctual thing.

If a man has the need to be taken care of and his wife doesn't understand it, avoids or denies it, or refuses to respond in any way, he's likely to feel a sense of loss or unhappiness—even though he may be unaware of exactly why. Somewhere inside his psyche he wants to know that his wife is willing to do things to make his life more comfortable.

Nurture or Nature?

I know; I know. You're absolutely right to be wondering at this point, "What about me?" I'm sure you'd too feel happy to have clean socks without having to do the laundry, so you might well be asking why your husband doesn't do that for you to nurture your needs.

He definitely should nurture your needs too, but there are reasons that a man, more than a woman, needs to be shown how to do that through his mate's example—and those reasons are rooted in both nature and nurture philosophies.

Most men are raised by women who take care of their domestic needs. They grow to expect this kind of caring from the women who love them. Most guys I work with identify their mothers as their main nurturer in their childhood; few of those guys had been encouraged in their upbringing to be caregivers.

"Hold on a minute," you say. "Girls are raised by women too, and they too get their socks washed by their mothers. So why don't they grow up looking for that same kind of care and attention from their mates?" Good question, and one good answer points to estrogen. There's evidence that females are wired to be the ones who have more to give emotionally. In one study, one-day-old females responded more strongly than males to the sound of a human in distress. One-week-old baby girls, but not baby boys, can distinguish an infant's cry from other noise, and four-month-old girls, but not boys, can distinguish photographs of those they know from those they don't know.[1] I just don't believe that these infants "learned" how to play gender roles as early as the first day of life. I think the difference is hardwired.

As they grow, girls are five times more likely to play with dolls, and much of their imagination is tied into tending to their "baby." Compare this to how boys play with their action figures, and I'm sure you'll agree that caregiving is much more natural to girls.

These findings and others quite similar indicate to me that right from birth, females have a more highly developed intuitive sense—they are gifted at reading the feelings and thoughts of others, detecting emotional clues, and responding in appropriate ways. Until the last two generations, most career women were in teaching or nursing—two very giving professions. Some say women gravitate to these types of careers that are extensions of the maternal role; others say that women have been relegated to them. Either way, there is a strong cultural and social history behind women's role as the caregiver.

For the happily married woman, whether the who-takes-care-of-the-home conflict is due to biology or upbringing doesn't really matter. What matters is whether her husband has a strong need to be taken care of by his wife. Is it part of his nature to need a wife who is willing to wash his socks, take his temperature when he's sick, soothe his hurts, and, yes, baby him when he needs extra attention? If it is, his wife will need to meet that need without feeling resentful if she is to remain one of the happily marrieds.

The Kindness That Goes Around Comes Around

If your gut reaction to the idea that your man needs you to take care of him is a negative one because you feel it puts an unequal burden on you, I concede that on some days, "You've got two hands, wash your own dirty socks" is a perfectly legitimate comeback. But at the same time, I'd have to ask you to take a careful look at what you're calling an "unequal burden." Do you really split all work equally? Do you do the typically "men's work" around your home—yard work, car repairs, plumbing and electrical repairs, and the like? What about the ultimate responsibility to provide enough money for food on the table and a roof over the head? Although there are households in which the wife tackles this responsibility, most men still take on this duty to provide as their own. Happily married women know that pulling out the who-does-what-when mental scorecards does nothing to improve the quality of marriage. Instead, they focus on how man and wife can balance out each other.

In my clinical practice, I find this manly need to feel cared for usually centers on domestic things. Men aren't saying, "Gee, I feel really annoyed that my wife never changes the oil in my car" or "How come my wife never mows the lawn?" or "Why can't my wife earn more money than me and take primary responsibility for supporting the family financially?" But they may very well be feeling, "It's so nice to have clean socks without having to do the laundry myself," or "Wow, I'm glad you thought of picking up my favorite ice cream at the store." This isn't simply an issue of the division of labor; these are the

REMEMBER THIS
You Are No Doormat

If you find that you're doing all the domestic work *and* all the men's work (or your husband has been hiring someone else to do his share), then it is time to sit down with him and sort through how domestic tasks are accomplished. Any man who wants a wife who will do *all* the work required to make a household run is bound to have to deal with any unhappiness that comes with that expectation. Or a husband who works at home in his art studio while his wife works a fifty-hour week in corporate America, who expects his wife to come home, make a great meal, and wash those socks, may need to adjust his expectations. In cases like these, it's time to rethink the division of household chores in a way that can meet his desire to be cared for but also meet the wife's need to feel like more than a household servant. If, for example, your husband pays a landscaper to mow the lawn, it's time for you to begin paying someone to do the laundry and ironing. Restore some equilibrium, without going on strike. The goal is happiness, not war.

kinds of things that nurture a man and make him feel happy and content in his marriage.

That's why women tend to be happier in their marriages when they understand that (1) men are not intentionally using them to do the dirty work, (2) men's expectations have grown out of their upbringing as well as social, cultural, and evolutionary processes, and (3) men can learn how to be more giving through their wife's example.

That's the bonus: Your actions can show your husband how to care for *you*. As you cater to your guy, he's watching and learning what marriage means. He's enjoying the love and care of his wife and will soon feel, if he doesn't already, the desire to do the same for you. It's human nature. We all tend to be kind and giving—in our own way—to those who are kind and giving to us. Your husband will return the kindness in ways that fit his nature, and, unfortunately for some women, that will never involve doing the laundry.

MEN NEED ACKNOWLEDGMENT FOR THEIR EFFORTS

Soon after the publication of my first book about happily married men, a book club group in rural Rhode Island invited me to attend a discussion of my work. To begin, the hostess of the group, Louise, shared a story about her husband that perplexed her. It seemed that Jim would help carry the groceries in from the car *if* she asked him, but he did it in a dramatic way. "He'll pile bag upon bag in his arms and place them on the kitchen counter with a loud grunt," said Louise. "And then he stands proudly in front of the grocery bags as if he had actually just gone out and hunted the food, slaughtered it, and dragged it across the jungle to place it on the table!"

All the women laughed because they recognized the same need in their own men to be thanked for doing routine household chores. "My Bill," added Julie, "expects me to pin a medal on his chest every time he watches the kids on a Saturday afternoon." Again, all the women laughed and nodded in agreement.

The actions of these men made perfect sense to me—probably because I'm a man. The many magnificent statues of great men that dot all the major cities of the world attest to the fact that men don't strive only to achieve: They want to be acknowledged for their achievements. They like people to connect with them on the basis of what they've done to make the world (or at least their home) a better place. This is a need that we still see in men in their marriages today—which in this age of gender equality is often misunderstood and criticized.

Of course, all of us, male and female, want to be recognized for what we do, but for most men, the need is greater. The real reason Louise's husband stands proudly in front of the grocery bags is that he wants Louise to say, in one form or another, "Thank you so, *so* much. I could *never* have brought in those groceries without you."

Okay. Okay. Yes, this kind of seemingly childish need is bound to give you a good laugh—probably good enough to knock you off your chair. After all, you too work hard day in and day out, and you don't expect anyone to pin a medal on you. Well, dust yourself off and settle back down in your seat, because I'm going to share with you something that may seem plain silly, but that will help you better know and love your man: It's quite possible that your husband is one of many men who need to feel like a hero.

The bottom line: Your husband may think he's Superman and you're Lois Lane. He's Spiderman; you're Mary Jane. You get the idea. You can laugh about it if you want, or you can outright ignore it, but if you treat your husband like someone who has helped save your life, he'll be motivated day in and day out to swoop in and do it over and over again.

When your husband performs an act of service, don't just say "Thanks." Say "THANKS!" Give him a hug (men tend to communicate with action). It would not take much time or effort for Louise to say, "I really appreciate your help; it makes my life so much easier." In this nanosecond, she will have motivated him to offer help again in the future, and he will more than likely do it without being asked.

You may be doubtful that such a strategy will work to get a guy to see things your way. Or perhaps you just don't want to play this game. But consider a situation that I see quite commonly: a married man leaving his wife for his secretary. A common reason men fall for their secretaries is that these women look up to them and satisfy their unmet need for acknowledgment. They see their boss as fighting a battle against stupid managers, incompetent workers, or irate clients. In other words, they worship their hero, and this is amazingly appealing to the men who are the objects of their awe. Ultimately, the once lowly clerical assistant now steps up and volunteers for the role of Lois Lane.

Some women have told me that they think this is a silly way to treat a man. But it's not just me—a man—who says that playing to the male's need for acknowledgment is a quick route to happiness. Amy Sutherland, an intelligent and insightful reporter for the *New York Times*, wrote an article titled "What Shamu Taught Me About a Happy Marriage" that says the same thing. In her engaging and witty style, she explains that while writing a story about how animal behaviorists get wild

Psst!

° Sharing a Secret

Get More Attention by
Giving More Attention

I've learned that when my husband makes even the slightest gesture of affection (even if it is as simple as "you look cute today") I need to go overboard showing my appreciation of his attention. I went for a year and a half of telling my husband I needed more affection from him (I even told him flat out that I wanted him to tell me I was beautiful). He did not respond to those demands and expectations. But one day, when he paid me an unexpected compliment, I stopped what I was doing and hugged him and kissed him and told him how much that meant to me. I began to do that every time he did something nice for me and guess what? He pays a lot more attention to me now. I hear that I am beautiful almost every day along with plenty of "I love you" and "You are the best thing that has ever happened to me." Men are not always thoughtful in the ways women want them to be. If you want him to make an effort to do things for you that don't come naturally for him, then you need to make it rewarding for both of you.

—Jaclyn, married 5 years

animals to do exactly what they want them to do, she realized that the same techniques would work on "that stubborn but lovable species, the American husband." "The central lesson I learned from exotic animal trainers," she concluded, "is that I should reward behavior I like and ignore behavior I don't. After all, you don't get a sea lion to balance a ball on the end of its nose by nagging. The same goes for the American husband."[2]

Reward behavior I like and ignore behavior I don't. Sounds like a model for happiness to me. I've seen the results over and over again. In fact, freely giving praise and thanks while refraining from nagging and complaining is one of the strategies that helped Rosa to get Lucas to *want* to change. It had never occurred to her to praise the very thing that was coming between them—his overtime work hours. Yet that's exactly what Lucas, like many men, wanted. Hearing a woman say, "I appreciate how hard you work" can make a man weak at the knees; it makes it much easier for him to hear her requests that he join her for dinner the following night. This is a far better tactic to make a man want to change than Rosa's either-or strategy that was forcing her husband to choose overtime work or his marriage. A man who feels that his efforts are appreciated is far more likely to get out of work on time so he can race home to his wife's smiles and words of affirmation. Ultimately, that's exactly what happened.

MEN HAVE TROUBLE VERBALIZING LOVE AND REGRET

Men are raised on such life lessons as "Talk is cheap. Action is key." This kind of training, combined with the male's brain circuitry, sets up the male of the species to be a creature of action rather than words.

Certainly, men can learn to verbalize their feelings and to respond better to the feelings of others, but such behavior doesn't come naturally. Part of the brain bridge that connects the right (emotional interpretation) and left (verbal exactitude) sides of the brain is less developed in men than in women. This doesn't mean that a man's right brain is weak. He can still apply intuitive and emotional thinking skills that help him solve problems through hunches. His left brain is also working fine, so his linear, logical, and sequential skills are in full gear.

The problem is that this structural difference may make it harder for him to use both lobes of the brain at the same time. When pressured to speak, men default to their dominant left lobe—the side controlling literal, not emotional content. Researchers in the area of gender communication express it this way: Men talk to *report,* whereas women talk to build *rapport.*[3]

Knowing this puts you in a better position to understand that the way your man expresses love and regret will be different from the way that you do. Then you can lovingly help him to appreciate what *you* are looking for from him; why you need to hear those words and how he can say them without giving up his manhood. (Those how-tos will also be explored in the next chapter and in Chapter Four's discussion of how to communicate with your man.)

A Woman's Way: With Words

You may be surprised to hear that any human being needs lessons on how to say "I love you" or "I'm sorry." You, with your more highly developed ability to put your emotions into words, probably feel very comfortable and confident with both of these expressions. But if your husband is like so many of the men who come to my office and who write to me on my Web site, he is going to be far less able than you to express these emotions verbally.

Let's start with expressions of love. It is very likely that you tell your husband how much you love him with words that sound like this: "I love you."

That's easy for you to say. Remember, you have more nerve cells in the left half of the brain where language is processed. And with your more fully developed pathways between the two brain hemispheres, you are better able integrate information from the logical (left) brain with the intuitive (right) brain.

For a lot of men I know, however, it's really difficult for those words to pass from their lips in a manner that does not seem to them forced or phony. It's often a response that they feel has been demanded and extracted from them like a sore tooth, and the words are difficult to enunciate. No kidding. Some men get hot and flushed, tongue-tied, and clumsy with their lips when they feel coerced to say these words: "OK, I looove you. I love yooo. Sure, I luv ya." All kinds of weird sounds come out in a rush. Some husbands will tell you that— if they are honest.

Meanwhile, you, far more than your guy, are both biologically and culturally reared to seek intimate connection. You, with your need to feel connected in a relationship, may talk with him about the events of the day. You, with your desire for connection, may sit staring into his eyes as you linger over a cup of coffee. You, with your romantic spirit, may arrange for a starry-eyed dinner with wine and dim lighting.

Unfortunately, he may not think to do any of those things to express his love for you.

In the same way, when it comes to saying "I'm sorry," you will usually do this the easy way by simply saying so. But many men will not. Communication expert Deborah Tannen points to a primary reason why these words are sometimes freely given by women but withheld by men. She has found that women often use the phrase "I'm sorry" in a complementary fashion. If a woman wishes an apology from a female friend, then she knows that sometimes she has to extend an olive branch first. Her friend recognizes the wish for reconciliation and responds in kind. Recognizing that women talk to build rapport, Tannen sees mutual apology between women as totally natural.[4]

So when a woman turns to a man and expects an apology, particularly if she offers one herself, she's often shocked, disappointed, and confused about why her man is too stubborn to offer the same in return. But spend a few moments in a man's frame of mind, and you may understand why this is so.

A Man's Way: With Action

Besides the general difficulty that many males have making the right brain talk with the left brain so that they can access both emotion and language at the same time, there is another reason that they tend to avoid such phrases as "I love you" and "I'm sorry." It is because of a heartfelt belief that talk is cheap.

"What good does it do to say these things?" they reason. "It doesn't change a thing."

"Anyone who feels that way should show it, not talk about it." Spoken like a man. Saying "I'm sorry" "or "I love you" just seems like an easy way out for men, and they won't insult you by even trying.

But don't lose hope. Your husband may be expressing his emotions in ways that you haven't been hearing. They won't come from his mouth. They will come from his actions.

He may not often say the word "love," but look for romantic expressions in the things he does for you. When he fills up your car's gas tank or picks up your clothes at the cleaners or cooks you a meal, he may be doing these things to show his love for you. Instead of sitting down and talking with you about feelings, he may see his hard work as a source of support and a gift to you. Romantic? Not by a woman's standards, but to many men, doing things for their wives is what love is all about.

"I'm sorry" is often expressed in similar ways. After you have an argument with your husband over something that is obviously his fault, instead of waiting for the words "I'm sorry," watch for the message in his actions. You may see him quietly

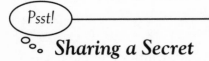

Sharing a Secret

"A Man of Few Words"

My husband is a man of few words and sometimes that drives me crazy. But I have found that I deal with that part of his personality much better when I remember that even though he says few words, they are usually carefully chosen and therefore hold more intent and substance than I initially realize.

—*Susan, second marriage of 10 years*

polishing your car or emptying the dishwasher. *Doing* something for you may be his way of expressing regret.

In fact, saying "I'm sorry" can be a much harder challenge for some men than saying "I love you." For men, talk (like so many interactions) is about hierarchy and one-upmanship. So when a man apologizes, he doesn't look at it as a way of bonding (as a female does); he looks at it as losing stature.

Take it from me: for a guy, that's major. You may be tempted at this point to say, "Grow up!" But I'm not here to reform men. I'm just here to explain them. Suffice it to say that one reason some men won't apologize is that they don't want to feel like less of a man—even though they are sorry.

One couple who was recently talking to me about infertility issues illustrated this method of apology. George didn't want to see a specialist; Loretta did. After a heated discussion, it became abundantly clear how hurt Loretta was by George's stone-cold refusal and how important this life step was to her. He never said he was sorry, but the next morning, when she went off to work, he called the fertility doctor and scheduled an appointment.

Loretta was touched by George's actions and told him so: "I'm sorry for the cruel things I said to you last night," she said as soon as he told her what he had done. "Thank you for understanding." And then to herself she added, "and because you made that phone call today, I know that you're sorry too."

If Loretta continues to notice when George speaks his heart through his actions, without insisting that he say the words "I'm sorry," it won't be long before he realizes that apologizing is not a painful or shameful thing. And when that happens, he'll start to open up and begin to verbalize those words of love and regret.

Before you can get your guy to speak his heart to melt your own, try to *see* his feelings of love and regret, accept this method of expressing emotions, and let him know that you understand the message.

MEN NEED TO PROTECT THEIR FAMILIES

Throughout the history of humankind, males have been assigned the role of protector. Men are generally bigger and stronger than their wives (not always, but usually). They have put their lives on the line to keep their family members safe. Modern-day men still feel the primal pull to be the brave defender, but without a grizzly bear threatening at the door, they must find other ways to "save" the family; at the very least, they need to have some control in the family dynamic.

In generations past, the man's role as head of the family was unchallenged. One of the benefits of this unquestioned status was the respect it accorded the man. But in modern marriages, this role is less pronounced. Women have stepped up and found that they are generally quite capable of running the house and making important family decisions too—resulting in an equal partnership. But in this equal partnership, what happens to the man's ingrained need to protect and defend? Sometimes it gets in the way of marital harmony—*unless* you can understand where all that male stubbornness and obstinacy is coming from.

This confusion over the difference between protecting and getting in the way is especially common in the home, which the female often views as her domain. If you put the vase of fresh flowers on the kitchen counter and your husband moves it to the dining room table, would you be annoyed? If you want to use freshly grated parmesan cheese for your dinner party and your husband suggests the ready-made cheap stuff instead, would you overrule him? Most women would because they tend to control domestic issues. So how then can a woman keep the peace in her home by letting her man have some control in the family dynamic? In many homes this need simply goes unmet, and the men find themselves staying longer and longer at work, where they have that sense of power and control. But in homes where the insightful wife is willing to occasionally grin and bear it, happiness is her reward.

Let's consider the family dynamic of Larry and Diana, for example. Larry would often throw in a load of laundry to help his wife. But he soon learned that he did not do it the way Diana would do it (by choosing the correct water temperature, pretreating soils, and separating permanent press from cottons). So he started staying away from the laundry room.

"Why bother going to the effort if it's not going to make her happy anyway?" he asked me.

My wife tells me that there certainly *is* a right and a wrong way to do the laundry. And although Diana was right, she's also a smart woman who knows how to get what she wants. When she saw Larry backing away from the laundry pile, she realized that her criticism had worked against her and made him feel incompetent. She remembered the lesson about men needing acknowledgment and began to praise Larry's efforts and give him hugs of thanks. *Then* she eased into laundry lessons to help him help her. That way she didn't extinguish Larry's need to help his family and (even worse for her) lose the possibility of getting the help around the house that she would like.

And what about Juan and Anna? Juan calls his wife every night before leaving the office and asks if there is anything she needs from the store that he might pick up for her on the way home. Some days it's a loaf of bread or half gallon of milk; other days it might be an onion or a tomato. When he first started picking up a few things, he often arrived home with items that Anna wouldn't have purchased: white bread instead of wheat, whole milk instead of skim, red onion instead of white, and perhaps a hard, unripe tomato. But Anna quickly learned that when Juan asked what she wanted from the store, she could get it by being very specific. Being a straightforward kind of guy, Juan was happy to know exactly what his wife wanted—allowing him the joy of providing for her needs.

And then there's Evan and Natasha. Evan wants to be a good father to his newborn son, but sometimes he's worried that he's an inept parent. Natasha noticed that he felt this way most often when his own mother came to visit. In her need to make sure that the baby was properly cared for, the new grandma would hover over Evan as he held the infant, saying

Guyness Quotient Quiz

How Would Your Guy Answer?

What, in your opinion, is the most reasonable explanation for the fact that Moses led the Israelites all over the place for forty years before they finally got to the Promised Land?

a. He was being tested.

b. He wanted them to really appreciate the Promised Land when they finally got there.

c. He refused to ask directions.

such things as, "Be careful. That's not how you hold a baby. You're going to hurt him. Hold his head more firmly and a bit higher up." This tore at Natasha's heart. Her mother-in-law was right, but the look on Evan's face when he thought that his incompetence might hurt his own son—the child he needed to protect more than anything else in life—was something she couldn't just ignore.

Natasha told me that on the day her mother-in-law commented about the proper way to hold the baby, Natasha stepped in and gently repositioned the baby in Evan's arms and then smiled at him, praising him for loving his son so much that she could see it in his eyes.

"I don't want Evan ever to feel that he isn't a good dad and provider, and I certainly don't want him to stop helping me because he thinks he does it wrong. We're both new at this, and although I do think I have better natural instincts as a parent, I know that I can't push Evan away without hurting him deeply. He needs to be a part of our son's life, and I'm going to patiently show him how."

With wives like Diana, Anna, and Natasha, these men are given opportunities to protect their families and keep them safe. I have no doubt that this is why they describe themselves as happily married men, why they speak so kindly about their wives, and why they will not disconnect from their families and wives by pulling away emotionally and absorbing themselves in their work, hobbies, or computer games as so many unhappily married men do.

It's in a man's nature to look for ways to protect his family. In these modern and less dangerous times, happily married women recognize and acknowledge the many, often inconsequential and even unhelpful attempts their men make to be involved, important, and manly.

MEN NEED TO BE RIGHT
AND IN CONTROL

The competitive drive ingrained in males over millennia has pushed them to achieve and triumph. It also is the reason they will fight to win an argument and won't easily back down if they think they are right (and sometimes even when they know they're not!).

Part of this is hormone related. We know that it's testosterone that makes men aggressive, and men have a lot of it, more than women. In addition, the hormone vasopressin (the male version of oxytocin, which is associated with feelings of attachment) promotes territoriality. It's one of the reasons men are more inclined to "stake a claim" about arguments of fact.

This aspect of the male's nature seemed to be causing turmoil in the household of a couple I had been seeing for several months. These middle-aged parents of a teenage boy arrived at my office one day barely talking to each other. As the story unfolded I learned that it was time for their son to choose a sport at school, and, as fate would have it, he just wasn't a natural athlete. Dad thought that his son should join the golf team because golf would combine definable goals with a feeling of teamwork. Mom, however, sided with her son, who preferred weightlifting. This wasn't just a disagreement; this was a *disagreement!* What made this particular discussion so intense was that in the past, Tim had rarely ever vetoed his wife's parenting decisions. But now, according to Debra, he wouldn't listen to reason.

So which sport did their son sign up for? I'll get to that. But first let's talk about why it was so important for Tim to make

REMEMBER THIS
It's All About Knowing Your Man

Writer Jonathan Alter crafted a very moving story for *Newsweek* about his experience with cancer. Describing the days after his diagnosis of lymphoma, he said:

> By this time I was in mental free fall. Friends later said I handled it courageously, but they were wrong. American culture rewards cheerful stoicism, a quality that cancer patients usually display in public but find difficult to sustain in private, especially at the beginning. I collapsed in tears only briefly, but retreated into a fog of unshakable misery. My detachment alarmed Emily, who wisely resisted many well-intentioned efforts by family and friends to coddle me. She understood that their instinct to be protective was making me into a weaker person than I needed to be. So she lovingly but firmly pushed me back into some semblance of normal life. "Get off the Internet and get back to your real work!" she insisted on more than one occasion.[5]

Isn't it beautiful how his wife knows him well enough to figure out how to get through to him and how to improve their lives through her actions and words? That's what marital happiness is all about.

a stand this time. Most men I talk to say that they don't really care all that much about many of the things their wives do. Their wives will show them color samples for the living room wall, and they'll shrug and barely respond. Men tell me that they'll be asked about what teacher their child should pick for kindergarten, and they'll . . . well . . . shrug and barely respond. You get the idea. There are many things that guys simply don't care about. But there are many things they do care about, and when a man has a strong attachment to an idea, he becomes possessive about it and is willing to fight to have his position accepted.

Men tend to separate out the emotional from the logical and sequential aspects of an issue. So when they register a

⁰°₀ *Sharing a Secret*

"Accept Your Husband as He Is"

Either wives have unrealistically high expectations or husbands are just lug nuts. Maybe it's a little of both. :-) But the bottom line is: If you want to be happy in your marriage, accept your husband as he is because he is not going to change fundamentally nor should he. Do not make him feel like a failure because he cannot live up to your expectations. Decide from the start that not only will you not be disappointed, but you will be happy and celebrate who he is and the way he is different from you.

—Mara, 47, married 28 years

"fact," they are not as likely as women to see that information as open to discussion. With less gray matter and more white fibers channeling brain cells to each other, men see things very clearly from *one* point of view—theirs.

So how did Tim and Debra settle things? Well, in this particular case, this dad was not going to concede his choice. When Debra realized how important it was to her husband to steer their son toward a more social sport and how determined he was to have his way, she was willing to concede, for the sake of marital unity, that there was value in her husband's point of view.

"My husband knows sports; he knows our son; and he needs me to trust him on this. So that's what I'm going to do," she told me, and then added, with that knowing smile that I've seen on so many wise women, "I guess I owe him this one."

MEN NEED ACTION

Caitlin is married to a guy who can't sit still—but this isn't a problem for her.

"Gosh no," she says with a wonderfully hearty laugh. "When Derek can't get rid of his pent-up energy, I can feel the tension in the house. I'd much rather have him get out and blow off some steam with his friends. When he comes home, he's so much more relaxed. That's good for both of us."

Some men do have an inborn need to be active. In general, men have greater muscle mass than women and are more likely to use physical activity to express their inner world *and* to relieve anxiety. For instance, we know that boys are ten times more likely than girls to be hyperactive. We recognize that boys have lower attention spans than girls in the school yard, and are more prone to play with action-oriented toys.[6] Now that he's grown from boy to man, your husband's need to move hasn't disappeared. That's probably why men, more often than women, are involved in such physical activities as playing on baseball, softball, or basketball leagues, coaching Little League teams, or working out at the gym. (Yes, women do these things too, but not as many of them and not as often as men.)

Wives can easily misinterpret this need to get out of the house as a need to get away from *them*, which leads to marital friction. But wives like Caitlin, who have men who are driven to get up and get going, don't try to tame that inner Tasmanian Devil, but rather support that aspect of their husbands' nature and reap the benefits—of which there are many. When a man has an opportunity to be physically active,

He's focused. When your husband can be physically involved in something, he is able to better exercise those powers of concentration that males are known for, and thereby to reduce his level of inner tension. That's why men particularly like physical activities that are goal oriented, structured, and linear—think of baseball and golf, or even household jobs like building a new fence, chopping firewood, or doing any constructive project that requires both physical movement and single-minded focus.

He's creative. When a man can move in space, he opens his body *and* his mind to the world in ways that are unpredictable and new. By experiencing changes in his bodily sensation and, especially where outside activity is concerned, by exposing himself to sights and sounds of the

REMEMBER THIS
His Marriage May Save His Life

Guys do love action—sometimes to the extreme. The male-only Y chromosome causes the brain of the fetal male to grow extra dopamine neurons. These nerve cells, involved in reward and motivation, propel boys toward thrill-seeking behaviors, and their extra dose of testosterone feeds their sense of fearlessness and adventure.[7] A study of preschoolers at a zoo found that the boys were about twice as likely as the girls to pet a burro, ride an elephant, climb a steep hill, or walk on the narrow ledge.[8] Any mother raising a young boy knows all about this "fearless gene."

Unfortunately for harried wives, this recklessness in males continues through every stage of development. Males, far more than females, participate in such extreme sports as deep-sea diving, ice climbing, parachuting, and downhill mountain bike racing.[9] Men are far less likely than women to fasten their seat belts when driving, and are more often the ones who will speed, tailgate, and refuse to yield.[10] And (not surprisingly) men are far more likely to die from accidental injury.[11] But again, you have the ability to make your guy a better man. Studies show that men who are married have much lower incidents of reckless driving, DUIs, speeding, and accidents.[12]

environment, your husband is more open to new ideas, less rigid, and more creative.

He's learning. Most men are more apt to learn about things by getting physically involved with them. That's one reason they aren't inclined to reach for an instruction booklet when they get a new power tool. First, a guy will test it out, try it on a few things, and, when he begins to run into a roadblock, then (and only then) he'll unfold the directions. Being physically active is how men learn about the world and their place in it.

If being active is an important part of your man's nature, you can see why making small changes to accommodate his passion for movement would be a good idea—and you can work it so that you get more of what you want at the same time. In fact, you can actually build emotional connection by joining in.

Let's say you've planned this coming weekend so that you and your husband can clean out the hall closet and then research used-car prices for your teenage daughter. There's nothing there that would nurture your hubby's need to get out and do something physical. So in the interest of improving the happiness quotient in your marriage, you might figure out a way to encourage your husband to get to work on that closet so that the two of you will have time to exercise, fish, hike, bike, play tennis, explore museums, or whatever you can think of that requires physical movement and not too much talk. Routinely spending time together outside the house is fun (with or without kids in tow) and provides good soil for emotional roots to grow. It's worth rushing through those "must-do" tasks on your weekend agenda in order to put the drudgery of domestic life behind you both for a little while.

On other occasions, you might even want to send him out to get his fill of activity without you. Although spending time in the great outdoors (or on the tennis court or at rock climbing in the gym) with your husband is good for your marriage, there are some times when you don't have to join in—in fact, your husband might even prefer that you don't.

Men need to play. And, despite the non-PC nature of it, sometimes it's just more fun when women aren't around. I like to go to tournaments for a card game called "Magic, the Gathering." I enjoy cross-country skiing. I don't think I'd mind if Susan chose to join me in my playtime, but, truth be known, I'm extremely self-absorbed and competitive, so I know that doing these things as a couple would not be that much fun for either of us. When my wife gives me space to ski or play Magic alone, I feel better, perform better, and am more relaxed and physically fit. And happier.

MEN HAVE AN UNDENIABLY STRONG ATTRACTION TO WOMEN

When I began my research into gender issues, I talked to many men who are deeply involved in the men's movement. For the most part, the participants of the discussion groups are great guys, and they have given lots of intelligent thought to some very deep issues. It occurred to me as I learned more about these men that in one very special way, they are different from their mirror image, feminists.

One of the most famous quotations attributed to Gloria Steinem and still seen today on T-shirts is "A woman needs a man like a fish needs a bicycle." Now, not all feminists see men as useless, but for many years the women's movement was not kind to our gender. What I noticed about the men's movement, in contrast, is that men *love* women. They genuinely, deeply, passionately think women are wonderful creatures. Okay, of course some of the guys don't like one particular woman (like an ex-wife), but generally they are intrigued by women and relish the role that women play in their lives.

Maybe men like women because they never really detach from their mothers; maybe they like women because pheromones unconsciously stimulate attraction. Probably, men have a biological imperative to reproduce, and seeking out women may be nature's way of perpetuating the species. I've heard it argued that individuals sense the parts of another's DNA chain that complements what is missing in their own. I've read texts that say we seek that which we were unable to obtain from our parents during our formative years. I give up tying to figure it out. But take it from a man who has made a career of listening to what men say about women: Women have a mesmerizing effect on men. That's why you may worry when your husband goes away on a business trip and why you sometimes watch to see if his eyes follow a beautiful woman as she walks past. He can't help being attracted to women—women are magnets to a man's nature. So why not use this undeniable allure to your advantage! Don't forget that especially as a married woman, you still have power over him—if you choose to use it. You can still charm your husband into supporting your interests by appealing to his own need to feel connected to you, his beloved wife whom he wants to please and to have as his happy partner forever.

This is one strategy that Michelle uses all the time with her husband, Rod. Michelle knows she can get things that matter to her by making Rod feel important and valued and, yes, sexy. For example, let's say Michelle wants to spend the evening with her girlfriend, but worries that Rod might not like being left behind. She doesn't see Rod's needs as signs of any deep character flaw. She's smart enough to know that the only reason he would feel that way would be if he thought she cared more about her girlfriends than she cares about him. That's what makes a guy feel slighted, she rightly assumes, not the evening out with a friend.

So to meet his need to know he's important to her, she'll use something she knows will ease his mind—her femininity. Before she goes out, she'll spend some undistracted time with

---

Psst!

°°∘ *Sharing a Secret*

"Something . . . Causes Our Eyes to Be Drawn to Women"

I was having an argument with my wife over why guys look at other women even when they are happy with the person they are with. My wife believes we as people have full control over whom and what we look at. It's my belief that men don't. We as guys have something inside, either chemically or instinctively, that causes our eyes to be drawn to women even if we are in love with someone else.
—Harry, 25, married 3 years

Rod. She'll sit by his side and tell him something positive: "I loved the way you looked in that new suit today—very handsome." Or perhaps say something sexy that will give him a reason to look forward to her return later in the evening—not in a manipulative way, but in a sincere and loving way.

A woman can soften the rough exterior of her husband's persona—and ultimately get exactly what she is looking for in her marriage—simply by being a woman. There is no shame in paying attention to what your man needs and wants to get happy! Using your feminine side is one more way you can nurture his nature.

A happily married woman is one who loves her man for who he is—not for who she wants him to be. Most will tell you that doing this is not always easy—but still worth the effort.

"There are times when my husband's view of life is different from mine," admits forty-three-year-old Marsha, "but when that happens, I have to remind myself that he's probably thinking the same thing about the way I view life, and that helps me put things in perspective. It's taken me time, but I've finally come to accept that the way he does things is not necessarily *wrong*, just *different*."

In the next chapter, we'll continue this discussion. Now that you know what a man's nature is all about, you can more easily nurture his needs—and make sure that he understands yours as well!

The Do Less Lesson

When you better understand the male and female mind and heart, you can do less pleading, yelling, and arguing; less complaining, worrying, and banging your head against the wall. When you stop trying to do it all, pick up his slack, make things even in all ways, and get him to do things the "right" way, you can spend more time laughing, hugging, and raising kids who see that Mom and Dad sure are different, but balance each other such that they can both thrive and be happy. In fact, you may come to the point where you don't see your husband's actions as shortcomings at all, but rather as expressions of otherness that attracted you to your guy in the first place.

To do less today, consider that lots of husbands tell me that they back off of parenting and household work because their wives criticize the way they do things. The critical approach doesn't seem to be working out for either wives or husbands, so I have a different proposal: give your guy another chance to let you do less today. Ask him to watch the kids for an hour or pick up groceries from the store or throw in a load of laundry. Then sit back and let him do it his own male way—no matter how wrong it may look to you, say nothing except "Thanks." In the end, he may not perform the task as well as you would, but hey— at least it's done. He's doing more; you're doing less. And that's bound to make you happy.

2

Nurture His Needs—and Yours

In the last chapter, we took a close look at the typical male—both his inborn nature and his social conditioning. In reality, no male is "typical"; only you can know the true nature of *your* man. To meet his deeply ingrained needs and help him better understand yours, you'll have to figure out which manly traits drive his behavior and view of life. This isn't easy because . . . well, he's a man and you're not.

In my book *The Secrets of Happily Married Men*, I ask men to listen to their wives so that they can learn how to better meet their needs. So too, at this point in this book for happily married women, the easy route to better understanding your man's nature and learning to nurture his needs would be to ask him: What part of your nature do I not understand?

Unfortunately, in most households, that strategy won't work. Most men find it difficult to verbalize what they need (if they've thought about it at all). So asking your husband to talk to you about his needs just won't help. You'll need to figure this one out yourself without much explicit input from your hubby. But by using your ability to translate your husband's actions and to empathize, communicate, and connect with others, you can certainly find out what you need to know.

Picking through the common threads of a few of your arguments might be a good place to start. You are certainly already meeting many of your husband's needs, but the unmet ones are probably the ones that cause the endless squabbles. Ironically, when your husband is striving to maintain his own status quo, you may feel that his approach gets in the way of what *you* want. That's why so many disputes end with you throwing up your arms in exasperation, saying "You'll never change!"

If the conflict is rooted in a condition ingrained in him by nature or upbringing that you don't yet understand, you're right—things won't change unless you take a different approach to getting what you need—one that pays attention to his nature.

Remember, you can't get a sea lion to balance that ball on the end of its nose by nagging.

The following quiz will uncover the roots of both the good and the bad in your man's nature and will help you guide him past those pesky male traits that may be getting in the way of your marital happiness. With your help, your wonderful man can learn how to use the things that make him who he is in ways that remind both of you exactly why you fell in love.

Quick Quiz to Better Know Your Man

This quiz, built around the common male needs explored in the last chapter, will help you identify your man's nature. Certainly not all men have all these needs, so let's take some time to identify the ones that you see in your husband. It's far easier to understand his needs when you know what they are.

Rate each of the following statements with a number from 1 to 5, where 1 means you don't agree with the statement at all, and 5 means no truer words were ever spoken!

1. The man who needs to feel cared for

_____ When my husband gets sick, he becomes paralyzed and needy.

_____ When I'm on the phone or busy on the computer, my husband gets pouty and wanders around the house aimlessly.

_____ When the house is messy, my husband gets agitated until I start to clean up.

_____ My husband says that I soothe him when I hold him in my arms.

_____ *His Score*

2. The man who needs acknowledgment of his efforts

_____ My husband will get very quiet if I don't praise him when he pitches in around the house.

_____ As soon as my husband comes home, he has to tell me about all his accomplishments at work.

_____ When he finishes work in the yard, my husband gives me a tour to show me all that he did.

_____ When my husband wears new clothing that he purchased himself, he struts around until I notice it.

_____ *His Score*

3. The man who has trouble verbalizing love and regret

_____ My husband doesn't say "I love you" very often; when he does, he seems uncomfortable.

_____ When I try to sit down and talk to my husband about my feelings, he gets restless.

_____ My husband will rarely say "I'm sorry."

_____ My husband doesn't understand why I apologize to my friends, saying, "You have nothing to be sorry about."

_____ *His Score*

4. The man who needs to protect his family

_____ My husband gets irritated when my friends call and unload their problems on me.

_____ When we go on long drives, my husband makes sure the car is in good shape by checking gas, fluid, and air levels.

_____ When it snows, my husband gets up early to clear the driveways or walkways, or to clean off my car.

_____ My husband takes care of having life insurance and disability insurance in case anything happens to him.

_____ *His Score*

5. The man who needs to be right and in control

_____ When my husband is watching sports with his friends, he'll argue over whether the referee made the right call.

_____ When I challenge my husband's opinion, he becomes sullen or angry.

_____ My husband boasts or says "I told you so" when he's made a correct prediction about something.

_____ Whenever we watch TV, my husband has to have the remote in his hand at all times.

_____ *His Score*

6. The man who needs action

_____ My husband hates to be at functions or events where he has to sit still for any length of time.

_____ My husband is regularly involved with exercise or athletic activities.

_____ My husband is most relaxed when we do physical activities together.

_____ When we visit family, my husband usually finds projects to do or goes off to do an activity with other guys.

_____ *His Score*

7. The man who has an undeniably strong attraction to females

_____ My husband enjoys looking at women in men's magazines, "American's Top Model," or even Victoria's Secret catalogues.

_____ When we're at the beach, I can't get my husband's attention because his eyes roam!

_____ When I get undressed, my husband ogles me.

_____ My husband tries to charm the cute waitress when we're out to dinner.

_____ *His Score*

Scoring Your Quick Quiz

What's the verdict? Take the total score from each category and jot the number down here.

The man who needs to feel cared for   ____ His Score

The man who needs acknowledgment
of his efforts   ____ His Score

The man who has trouble verbalizing
love and regret   ____ His Score

The man who needs to protect his family   ____ His Score

The man who needs to be right and in
control   ____ His Score

The man who needs action   ____ His Score

The man who has an undeniably strong
attraction to females   ____ His Score

15 or more: That's pushing his buttons!

In which category of manly traits does your husband score the highest? Those that score 15 or more represent possible hot-button points. If you are aware that these needs are strongly motivating your husband's behavior, you'll be in a better position to find true marital happiness.

Between 12 and 15: Could be serious

If the tally is between 12 and 15, the trait is still worth paying close attention to. These may be strong attributes in your guy, and knowing this can help you better interpret his actions and comments. But they're not dyed in the wool, and you shouldn't assume that your husband is inflexible in these areas.

Between 8 and 12: Common ground
Scores that fall between 8 and 12 may tell you that your husband has some traits in an area, but they're not prime motivators. This gives you the opportunity to find considerable common ground with your mate; in many cases, you and he may actually handle situations in much the same way.

Less than 8: Not a concern
If the count is less than 8, it's likely that this personality category isn't a major source of conflict in the household. No need to put time and effort into understanding and nurturing this male trait. Your man's behavior is not motivated by it.

Remember, there's no good or bad in this test; some women report scores for their husbands higher than 15 in every single category! All that says is that these husbands were born with, developed, or were taught to have these typically male characteristics.

These are the elements of your husband's nature that make him who he is—the man you chose to marry. With these traits in mind, read on to find out what you can do to better love your husband by using your inborn capability to tend to his needs.

A THREE-STEP PLAN

Looking over the roots of the essential qualities of your man, you may notice that some are the very traits that attracted you to him in the first place: his manly demeanor, his ability to take control of a tough situation, his cool and calm attitude. Over time, however, those same traits can get quite annoying. But they do make him who he is. And fortunately,

REMEMBER THIS
A Revised Serenity Prayer

When you identify a need that is rooted in your husband's nature, and it's one that is causing friction in your marriage, remember the Serenity Prayer:

"God grant me the serenity to accept the things I cannot change, the courage to change the things I can, and the wisdom to know the difference."

This sentiment is a helpful guide for putting life in perspective, but in the case of happily married women, this prayer might better read:

"God grant me the serenity to accept the aspects of my husband's nature that I cannot change, the courage to direct his instincts in ways that will be mutually gratifying, and the wisdom to better understand who he really is."

Okay, maybe it's not as elegant at the original Serenity Prayer . . . but you get the idea.

as many happily married women have discovered, there are three simple ways to tend to his needs and get your own needs met as well:

1. Understand his needs.

2. Nurture his needs.

3. Negotiate around those needs.

Let's look at how this plan works.

Step One: Understand

Understanding a guy's nature often takes some investigative work, as forty-eight-year-old Carla discovered when trying to interpret the behavior of her husband, Dave, who is ten years her senior.

"I used to think that Dave was some kind of caveman!" Carla told me, shaking her head as she smiled at the thought. "I can't believe I misread him so completely."

"We'd have the same argument every time I wanted to buy something electronic—like an iPod or plasma TV or high-end cell phone or a Blackberry. 'We don't need it,' he'd say. I thought that was his way of saying 'I'm too cheap to spend any money.' I feel terrible now that I didn't catch the meaning behind his words."

A week earlier, I had asked Carla to tell me other ways in which Dave was stingy with money; she was stuck for an answer. It turns out that Dave does spend money freely on other things, like cars and vacations; in fact he had recently bought Carla a beautiful necklace just because he saw it and knew it would make her happy. He didn't sound like a cheap guy to me.

Assuming Dave was not really a caveman and that the couple did have indoor plumbing and a TV, I asked Carla if there might be some other reason Dave resisted buying *electronic* items.

"I can't figure him out," she admitted. "He insisted that he did not want a microwave in our house—something about radiation—but then when my father bought us one for our anniversary, he seemed okay with it. After getting really angry about being overruled, he now loves it and uses it all the time.

My son bought us a DVD player, and we really enjoy it. He just won't buy this stuff himself."

"Is it possible," I asked Carla, "that your husband needs to feel in control of things?"

"Oh, absolutely!" she laughed.

"Is it possible that he doesn't want to bring electronic items into the house," I continued to wonder aloud, "because he's afraid he won't know how to work them and then feel foolish in front of you and the kids?"

"I guess so," she said with a soft laugh. "He really is not very high tech. He's still uncertain about how to use the computer; when we need driving directions or when he wants to get a stock quote, he always asks one of the kids to do it for him. Sometimes I get really annoyed that he doesn't do it himself, but maybe he doesn't know how. Wow! Why didn't

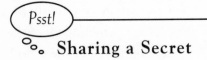

Sharing a Secret

"Step into Each Other's World"

Rather than focus on biological differences alone (and I do think many are valid), I would focus on unique-ness: what motivates each of us, what makes each of us come alive, what drains our energy. It is helpful and generous to step into each other's world and per-spectives, and be curious rather than judgmental, ask open-ended questions to find out what the other might be thinking and feeling.

—Andrea, 45, married 15 years

I see that? I should have realized that it must be embarrassing for him to be thrown into this high-tech world where he can't feel in control anymore."

Carla didn't see at first that Dave's need to be a knowledgeable expert who is in control was at the root of his refusal to buy electronics, because she was looking for the root of the problem in the wrong place. By nature, Dave isn't cheap with money, but he is a proud man. The problem was rooted in his self-image as someone who knows what he is talking about— someone who doesn't stare at a Blackberry with no idea what it does or how to make it work.

Knowing this, Carla has stopped feeling annoyed about Dave's "cheapness" and instead is working to teach him how new gadgets work. This week she borrowed a Blackberry from a friend to "play" with it for a while and then share the fun with Dave. Later this week, she's going to ask him to help her find that stock quote on the computer, just so he can watch how she does it.

More important, her empathy will now kick in and help her better understand why forcing electronics on Dave by, perhaps, buying him an iPod for his birthday will not make him happy—but instead embarrassed and even angry.

Understanding how your man's nature may be at the root of those quirky things he does that drive you crazy is a major move toward marital bliss for both of you.

Step Two: Nurture

The adage "give and you will receive" was probably first pronounced by a happily married couple who learned over the years that if you give to someone genuine happiness by catering to that person's needs (even when you don't always agree or fully understand), you are far more likely to receive kindness and happiness in return. And when your husband catches on that your marriage is based on a willingness to understand each other and to respect each other, it won't be long before his inborn desire to do the same for you blossoms—making your life a whole lot easier.

Empathic nurturing can also help avoid misunderstandings when the female way of looking at life collides with the male way. This kind of misunderstanding is what brought Sheila and Ken to my office.

Ken is the kind of husband who likes to help out at home. He often does the laundry before Sheila wakes up on Saturday mornings. Later in the afternoon he mows the lawn and takes the kids for ice cream so that Sheila can have some alone time. Sheila is a happily married woman, but for a long time she felt irritated at her husband, and failed to appreciate his efforts.

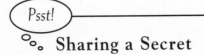

Sharing a Secret

"He might find ME annoying!"

I don't expect a perfect human being, and if he's doing great on the important stuff, the other stuff that annoys me are small potatoes. One thing I learned from my husband helps me put up with a lot: it never occurred to me that he might find ME annoying! Remembering this helps me keep things in perspective.

—Lynn, married 7 years

"Yes, he does all this wonderful stuff," she admitted at our first meeting, "but then ruins it by getting sulky in the evening. He'll almost always throw it back in my face with something like, 'I'm really tired after doing the laundry and the lawn and then watching the kids.' That's so aggravating. Does he want a medal for doing what he's supposed to do as a father and husband?"

Well . . . kind of. Ken obviously is a man with the deeply ingrained need for acknowledgment—that drive to do his best so that he can earn praise. Is this annoying from a woman's point of view? From the perspective of a woman who gives and gives to her family all week long, expecting no reward in return? Of course it is. But men like Ken are motivated by this quest for reward, so if that's what they need to keep doing the wonderful things they do (and making life easier for their wives), why not give it to them?

Ken wants a pat on the back for being a good husband. So (after rolling her eyes a few times at this "stupid" need) Sheila agreed to give it a try. During the following week, whenever Ken went out of his way to do something nice for her, Sheila made a point of acknowledging his effort: "Thanks for picking up the kids from sport practice; that helped me have time to get dinner going." When he took the kids to the park the following Saturday, she rewarded him with, "That two hours without the kids underfoot was a wonderful gift. Thank you."

Sheila was appealing to Ken's need for recognition. She was making him happy in a very simple way, and, by acknowledging his efforts to please her, she could rest assured that by evening Ken would not get testy and ruin the night for both of them.

Both are happy. But this is the part where some of my readers may be saying, "What happened to the 'do less' part for wives? Nurturing my husband's nature is a fine idea, but the plan has a strong potential to backfire if my man takes all my nurturing and understanding but gives back nothing. I don't see Ken acknowledging all that Sheila does to keep him happy. Won't Sheila end up feeling resentful?" Sure, it can happen. And women often have reservations about this appeasement idea. One woman, Karen, was very direct when she responded to one of my newsletters that advocated giving men a "high-five" for their work around the house, saying, "Please don't tell us to 'boost his ego.' That is like 1960s advice on 'how to keep your man.' If my man's ego isn't big enough when I marry him, all the boosting in the world isn't going to change it. It is his job to feel secure, sufficient, and sexy. It is an inside job. The biggest return on our actions comes from working on ourselves, not on our mate!"

Well, Karen, as far as I'm concerned, you can't take everything off the table. If both partners say, "I'm not giving you anything more than you give me," there is no happiness to be had. A happy marriage depends on the willingness of each partner to give, without keeping a tally. Moreover, it relies on a willingness to look for ways that your partner is giving to you, even if they are not overt. This is the smile across the room, the almost imperceptible touch as he walks past, the dish of ice cream while you're watching TV, the kiss good-bye and hello each day. These are all types of giving.

It may seem like hard work, sometimes, to give when you don't feel given to, but, as Sheila's example demonstrates, resentments stir up negative feelings, and you actually end up getting *less* of what you want. By nurturing Ken's nature,

Sheila encourages Ken to show her his love in the ways he knows how. Everybody wins!

Happily married couples know that happiness is not an inside job that each spouse creates for himself or herself—it is something that both partners give to each other each and every day of their life together.

Step Three: Negotiate

There will be times when your husband's needs clash with yours, and doing things his way is just not acceptable. But it's unlikely that there will be many issues on which you won't be able to find some common ground, as Jane did:

Carl, unlike his buddies, is a neat-freak. "That's putting it kindly," says his wife, Jane. "Carl grew up in a military family, and needs everything in its place before he can sit down and relax. So when he comes home from work, he does what I call his 'white-glove inspection' before he can enjoy the night. When we were first married, it was no big deal to keep the place clean. I kinda liked that he wasn't the typical slob of a guy who left his drawers on the floor. But now with two kids always making a mess, his need for cleanliness is driving me crazy!"

Although Jane understands that having a clean home is important to Carl, maintaining a spic-and-span household is now out of the question with children around. Carl is going to have to give a little on this.

The solution was negotiated in a very calm conversation after the kids went to bed: "I can't keep the house as clean as you want it to be anymore," Jane began with a direct assertion that she knew would get his attention. "I understand your need to have the house look in order, and I admire you for that. But now that the kids are running around making messes faster than I can possibly clean them up, I'm finding it too stressful to keep up the standard of cleanliness you have set.

"Something has to give, and here's what I propose: the downstairs rooms will be carefully cleaned when you come home, but the basement playroom and the boys' upstairs bedroom may not always be straightened up. Deal?"

In this conversation, Jane opened the way for talking about both their needs. Using her superior verbal abilities, she acknowledged his nature and explained her own feelings using the get-to-the-point vernacular he's accustomed to. By crediting his strengths, along with offering a middle-road solution, she found the key to successful negotiations and a happy marriage. Jane was able to understand Carl's needs, appease to a point, and then negotiate the rest.

Knowing and nurturing your guy's nature is a great way to get what you want out of your marriage, but it doesn't guarantee that there won't be arguments and misunderstandings. No, even happily married men and women have their occasional fight. In the next chapter, we'll take a look at how some women manage to fight and love at the same time.

The Do Less Lesson

Understanding and reacting to the core nature of your husband rather than to what a situation looks like from the outside will put a whole new spin on the way you react to him when he asks, "What's for lunch?"

It's no secret that saying, "Don't be so lazy; get your own lunch" isn't the comeback that leads to happiness. Knowing that he makes connections through action rather than words, you'll see that he's not necessarily saying, "I want you to wait on me hand and foot." He may simply be making an attempt to bond with you, to involve you in his life, to get back something he needs to feel connected. After you understand this and then work either unilaterally or together (maybe he's just waiting for a signal to make his own sandwich and eat together) to meet his needs, it will be far easier to get him to focus on your "honey-do" list. This is where you get to do less—less badgering, less arguing, and ultimately less of the stuff that he will now do himself.

POLITICS & PROSE

BOOKSTORE & COFFEEHOUSE

425327 Reg 1 ID 126 5:01 pm 12/22/08

S SECRETS OF HAPPIL	1 @ 14.95	14.95
SUBTOTAL		14.95
SALES TAX - 5.75%		.86
TOTAL		15.81
CASH PAYMENT		16.00
CHANGE		.19

Check out the Coffeehouse downstairs

3

Fight Better

Wanna fight!? Get married!

So start typical jokes knocking marriage. But I've been hearing from lots of women who approach the marital battle field in a refreshing way—women like Victoria, whose common-sense attitude about arguing is actually a boon for her marriage:

"I intend to stay married to my husband for the rest of my life—which is a very long time to expect any two people to be in total agreement on everything. So I know we're going to fight (we've had some doosies!). But when we're arguing, I try to remind myself that since we're in this for the long run, we're obviously going to make up eventually. That makes it easier for me to make up sooner rather than later."

If more couples accepted conflict as part of the marital package, there would be much more bliss in this world—and far fewer couples in my waiting room.

A typical scene in my office each day goes like this:

A couple walks in, sits down, and glances at each other rather guiltily.

"So what brings you here?" I ask.

"Well," one of them will say, bravely breaking the silence, "We love each other, but we argue a lot; we disagree on so many things."

My usual, nonjudgmental response is, "Join the club!" I honestly don't know what couples expect me to say to the complaint "We argue." The expectation that two people could possibly live together year after year and *not* argue is an unrealistic one. Given the simple fact that he's a man and she's a woman, there are plenty of reasons for misunderstandings and hurt feelings—and they're bound to happen even in the best of marriages.

So an important step in attaining a happy marriage is to accept the fact that sometimes you're going to get angry, furious even, at your husband, and still be in love and still stay together for life.

"But," some people have been quick to inform me, "we didn't used to argue. In the early days of our relationship, we always got along."

No doubt that's true. When a relationship is still in the early romantic stage of love, both parties have a strong desire to meet each other's emotional needs, and they tend to deal better with (or even ignore) the other's quirks and differences. Romantic love is blind! When conflict does occur in this stage, it's often quickly resolved because both partners are anxious to return to the good feelings and are willing to give in to get the relationship back on track. But as the relationship ages and you both move into the later stages of love, you start to get annoyed more easily, so conflict occurs more frequently.

And that's not necessarily bad. Research from the Center for Marital and Family Studies at the University of Denver found that couples who argue are more likely to be satisfied with their marriages than couples who withdraw from conflict.[1] That's because disagreements make you think about the relationship. Consider it this way: Every time you argue with your husband, it's just your relationship's way of saying, "Heads up; something's going on here that needs attention!" Arguing is one more technique you can use to find out what it is you both need from each other.

The women who seem unscathed after a marital dispute know that happy couples don't fight less—they fight better.

SMART MANEUVERING

In happy marriages, both partners contribute to the quality of the relationship *and* to the quality of the marital fights. So it's absolutely true that your husband too has a role to play in

REMEMBER THIS
Work from a Strong Base

Learning to improve your marriage by fighting better is a sound strategy when disagreements spring from differences of opinion and personality. If your marital arguments involve infidelity, addictions, mental illness, or domestic violence, the suggestions in this chapter may help you communicate better with your spouse, but you may also require individualized professional guidance.

fighting smarter. But research has found that even in the best of marriages, women are the ones who lodge over 80 percent of household grievances.[2] In less academic language: The wives are the first to speak up. This is probably because, if the studied marriages are anything like the marriages I see in my clinical experience, many men just don't seem to notice or be concerned about the things that women often use as barometers of marital satisfaction.

In fact, I'm convinced that's why so many men come into my office, throw their hands up, and say, "I don't know what to do to make her happy." As a man, I can say with some authority that men are often clueless about the things that start their marital arguments. They're shocked when their wives say, "You turn on that computer and then pay no attention to me" or "Why did you ask me if I was going to have a second helping of pie? Are you trying to tell me I'm fat?" They just don't see it coming, but are quick to react defensively once the gauntlet is thrown down.

Given the inevitability of conflict in a marriage and a man's often oblivious nature (until provoked), what's a wife to do? An awful lot of smart women learn very early in their relationships with men that if they know the male's strengths and weaknesses, they can develop an effective plan of attack or surrender that very often gives them the victory. That's not manipulative—that's smart tactical maneuvering on the part of the person known to most often make the first move.

While writing this section, I realized that I used some battle words and images—fighting, strategy, defensive, gauntlet, maneuvering, tactics, and surrendering. I hadn't intend to, but that's how guys think about conflict. To a man, a fight is something to be won.

MEN AND CONFLICT

Most men and women handle their anger in very different ways. When women are upset, they tend to open up emotionally and verbally. Researchers have shown that, when stressed, women are more likely to reach out to those around them and bond together as a way of managing rising tensions.[3] This "tend and befriend" instinct puts a premium on sharing words and feelings. It's a valid and effective way of dealing with conflict—unless your conflict is with a typical, battle-minded man.

A man tends to respond to stress with the fight-or-flight reaction: He feels an increase in blood pressure and pulse, and reacts to emotionally charged situations by shutting down verbal communication and narrowing his visual and mental focus. In other words, he loses his communication skills.

When men sense an argument coming, their body sends signals to the alarm center of the brain, the amygdala, which is responsible for engaging the fight-or-flight response. When this almond-shaped brain organ gets activated, it makes rational thought difficult, and all but the most emergent problem-solving abilities collapse. Sure, the amygdala is great for getting a guy to rush through a blazing fire to rescue his family, but it's not so hot for helping him think out how to demonstrate his complex mix of feelings when his wife gives him the silent treatment because he forgot to ask her about her very important job interview. Remember, he's good at showing his feelings through action, but may be less skilled at describing it with words. The less robust connections between the two sides of his brain make it tough for him to use his verbal left brain to talk about what's going on in his emotional right brain. That can make the female's method of verbal conflict resolution foreign to him. He needs his wife to show him, guide him, and teach him how to fight in a way that can work for both of them.

Let's take a sample case that seems simple on the surface, but holds explosive potential because it involves child care, priorities, misunderstood feelings, and even marital power issues.

In this hypothetical marriage, Jennie loves her husband, Jim, but hasn't yet learned how to use her superior listening and empathic skills to understand the male point of view and to get what she needs from him. Instead, she pushes all the wrong buttons, and soon it's all-out war.

Let's say that Jim comes home late even though he knows Jennie needs him to watch their son, Jason, while she goes to her night class. Jennie glares at Jim as she rushes past him saying, "You know how hard it is for me to work all day and then go to these classes at night! The least you could do is come home on time just once. Is that too hard for you? Once again, it's all about you!"

Jennie has a right to be angry, and she tells Jim exactly how she feels. From her point of view, her husband is selfish—he doesn't take her needs seriously, and she tells him so.

What Jennie doesn't know, because she made an offensive move that signaled "take your battle positions" before Jim had a chance to explain, is that Jim had a flat tire on the way home; he left his cell phone at work in his rush to get out the door, and he feels awful about making her late for her class. Unfortunately, she probably will never know what Jim's intentions were, because once a man is attacked, his inability to explain or express himself leaves him with three rather ineffective but typically male responses: (1) analyze, (2) attack, or (3) withdraw.

When Men Go Logical

Men are not born or raised to be touchy-feely responders. They are hardwired and then trained to find answers through logical analysis, not through emotion. When they are facing contradictory information, often their first reaction is to ask, How can this be solved with reason and logic? This makes them crackerjack problem solvers.

In contrast, when faced with the same conflict, a woman is more likely to be in touch with her immediate, emotional reaction that pushes her to focus on her feelings and focus less on objective evidence. This is a skill that serves her well in many aspects of her relationships with others, and she wants her husband to approach the situation in the same way. He will not.

So Jim is bound to miss the emotional roots of his wife's complaint and will instead try to defend himself in a very objective way against untrue accusations. Using his highly developed sense of reason, he might say, "Jennie, I don't do this all the time; I have come home on time many nights in the past. And as far as saying I care only about myself, well that's obviously just not true, since I work overtime three days a week just so you can have that vacation you want every year. And what about that time last summer when I bought you that nice watch. Who was I thinking of then?"

Well done, Jim! You've scored! You've just come up with a logical response to your wife's unfair complaint. Only one problem: This won't win you any medals, because you missed the point of your wife's anger entirely when you focused on setting the factual record straight.

If Jennie's still in the room after Jim's first go-round at fixing things, our hapless Jim is likely to make things worse with his next move, which will be to offer what he thinks is a logical solution. Missing the point that he has disappointed his wife and made her feel like a low priority (which is what she is really angry about), he will look for a solution to the babysitter problem instead. That, from his point of view, will surely show his wife that he does care about her situation.

"Instead of getting all upset if I'm late," he'll say, "why don't you ask our babysitter to come over until I get home?" We'd better stop rooting for Jim now, because this is not going to end well. Jennie sought to correct her husband's actions by demonstrating that she was upset with him. Now he's turned the topic all around: It is no longer a matter of whether or not he respects Jennie's wishes; rather, he is suggesting that she's wrong for getting upset. But the situation could get worse if Jim chooses to elevate the argument to the next level—the loud one.

When Men Attack

The male's higher level of testosterone and his school-yard training make him a challenging opponent for a female. Physiologically men are built with less astute hearing and stronger vocal and lung capacity than women. When a man doesn't have his logical brain to turn to, he may seek to make his perspective known by being loud, even bellowing. He has less acute pain sensations in his extremities; he may bang his fists on the table to make his point. He has higher muscle mass, which requires great amounts of circulatory capacity, and his body will swell with anger—showing bulging veins in his neck and a burning red face. Men's innate aggressive drive will surface. And, most remarkable from a woman's point of view, he is at ease with these feelings; they boost him up for that eternal king-of-the-hill battle.

The rules of the school yard, the athletic field, and the board room don't apply, however, when it comes to his marriage. Banging his chest from the mountaintop comes in handy in the wilds of primeval forests, but it's not welcome on Main Street, Anywhere, USA. Now he is expected to respond verbally to explain how he really feels. Jennie would like to hear Jim say something like, "I feel bad for you that you lost out on your chance to get to class on time. I want you to know that I care deeply about your needs." But because of Jim's body chemistry and social training, Jennie will probably never hear those words.

When Jennie expressed her anger at Jim, he felt assailed. If he chooses option 2, "attack," the fight-or-flight response ingrained in him since the dawn of time will kick in, and he's likely to roar something like, "You are so self-absorbed! You have no idea how hard I worked to get home in time, and all you do is complain!" His inability to comfort his wife (by empathizing with her emotional experience) makes him feel shamed—even guilty—so he lashes out. There will be no calm discussions once that happens.

This expression of anger sets off an alarm in females that locks a husband and wife in an uneven battle where male and female natures once again interfere with an easy resolution. Relationship experts Patricia Love and Steven Stosny tell us that females are programmed to sense danger and seek safety. In fact, they continue, a woman's primal need is to avoid fear.[4] So when a husband raises his voice or pounds his fists, his wife's fear stimulates her own adrenaline rush of the fight-or-flight response, and she will either retreat from the conflict or lash out in a bid for survival. If she begins to express deep emotions triggered by this trepidation, either by crying or attacking back, the fight may bump up another level, because any manifestation of her fear intensifies his feelings of shame.

Most men feel responsible or to blame when women are unhappy. In fact, lots of guys see their wives' tears as a sign of their own incompetence or even as a way for a woman to manipulate a man by daring him to prove he's good enough.

This is why arguments over the simplest things tend to escalate. The male is committed to defending himself against feelings of shame, and the female responds passionately to ward off the cause of her fear. Now the little tiff over who's supposed to watch Jason after work becomes an all-out war of yelling, banging, crying, and screaming. This is no longer about parental responsibilities; it's about lashing out with one hand and defending one's self with the other. Unless they can understand what's going on, neither side will give in. So the fight continues, with both sides feeling wronged.

When Men Withdraw

If a man chooses not to fight, he will choose flight—equally annoying to his wife. That's what's going on when your man storms out of the room and slams the door behind him. Discussion closed. You can run after him and try to get him to continue the fight—in hopes of getting his side of the story. But most often, once he's turned away from the debate, he's not coming back, and if you pursue the point, he'll end up leaving the house completely.

When he can't physically flee the room, he'll withdraw emotionally—making him appear controlling and arrogant. When he refuses to talk about a problem, you can try to badger him into conversation, dare him to defend himself, beg him to explain his point of view. But you're more likely to push him further into retreat than elicit a rational discussion.

In my experience, men who choose to stonewall an argument are often conveying a message that is quite different from the one their wives are hearing. To boost your level of marital happiness, stop and think the next time your husband withdraws from a fight. He might be saying:

I want you to see my point of view, but I can't put into words my strong feelings about why I feel this way, so I just won't say anything.

I feel so strongly about this that I can't debate it with you without losing my temper. I don't want to do that; I don't want to say or do things I'll regret, so I'm not going to talk anymore about it.

I know I'm right about this, but to avoid feeling guilty or feeling like I'm disappointing you, I have to pull away completely.

If you start tracking the way your husband reacts to the conflicts in your marriage, you'll see that when angered he's often logical, loud, or withdrawn—or a combination of all three, quite often in that order. If you know what to expect, you'll be prepared to deal with it.

TOP MARITAL CONFLICTS

There is no way to name or number all the issues that cause marital conflict. But as I sit each day listening to couples vent their marital problems and frustrations, five topics continually

REMEMBER THIS
About Domestic Violence

Although men don't report physical abuse because they're often ashamed to admit it, a collection of recent studies has found that violence against men is not as uncommon as some people think. And women are just as likely as men to be the first to initiate physical fighting, also with serious consequences.[5] Yes, violent men may cause more severe injury to women than abusive women inflict on their male partners, but violent women too are quite capable of severely injuring a man. Physical fighting has no place at all in a healthy marriage—for anyone!

rise to the top: (1) distribution of child care and housework, (2) sex, (3) money, (4) parenting, and (5) use of leisure time.

The issue of who does and does not help out around the house is a hot button that's so important to a happy marriage that I discuss it in detail in Chapter Six. Resolving sexual conflicts is also so vital to a happy marriage that I've given it its own chapter. See Chapter Five: "Have Lots of Sex."

I cover the third, fourth, and fifth areas of discontent—money, parenting, and use of leisure time—in this chapter. Sorry, but I cannot see into your life and know exactly how these issues affect you, your husband, and your degree of happiness. But I can give you a look at the ways in which these three issues commonly spark marital upset and how some women deal with them and come out happy on the other side.

Conflict 1: Fighting About Money

Conflicts about money are about more than dollars and cents. They are about upbringing, personal values, and relationship issues that go much deeper than the checkbook balance:

- Because the way a person handles money is some-times interpreted as the way he or she prioritizes all aspects of life, some spouses feel less important than the plasma TV.

- Because sometimes the way someone handles money defines his or her character, a frugal person may feel disrespected by a free-spending spouse who appears to be deliberately reckless.

- Because sometimes the way a person handles money projects an attitude about earning more or less than the Joneses, this fuels hurtful labels such as *selfish*, *greedy*, or *lazy*.

With so many different ways for money to cause hurt feel-ings and misunderstandings, it's no wonder that a third of 1,022 people recently polled said that a lack of financial responsibility hurt their relationships even more than their partner's being unfaithful. The national telephone poll also found that keeping the finances straight even trumped a good sex life—respondents were twice as likely to select financial responsibility (22 percent) over sexual compatibility (10 per-cent) as a personal trait that has sustained their relationships over the years. The survey also found that late bill paying was cited as often as problems with in-laws as a stressful situation that put pressure on a relationship.[6] Money matters!

We met Rosa in the first chapter. As a young wife, she struggled to understand what she thought was her husband's greed, which was driving him to work excessive overtime hours at the hospital while neglecting her. Remember that what drove him turned out to be something quite different—his need to provide for her and to feel successful and accomplished. Despite years of evolving economic equality that has made the two-income marriage the norm for most couples in the United States, many men, like Rosa's husband, Lucas, still feel responsible for providing for their families. (Yes, even men who earn less than their wives feel this way.)

To many of these men, money is the symbol of self-worth. It is a concrete sign of success. A few generations of female breadwinners are not going to breed this out of him. So when a wife complains about lack of money, a man's irritation is usually not directly related to the issue of money, but to his belief that his manhood is being attacked. I don't think there's a woman alive who has heard the words, "You're right, honey; I'm just not a good provider for our family" when they're not dripping with sarcasm or anger. Because a man attaches so much of his identity to the provider role, attempts to discuss financial problems may bring out feelings of shame or guilt in him. Don't be surprised if when pressed to explain why the coffers are dry, he brings out his logical, loud, or withdrawn side to protect himself from these bad feelings.

Even when the male's ability to provide for his family isn't in question, there are bound to be arguments over how the family money should be spent or saved. Over and over I've heard these kinds of complaints:

"She can't keep spending more than we make. Designer clothes and resort vacations are just not in our budget."

"He has plenty of money for a plasma screen TV, but none to send our kids to private schools."

"Why do we have to have these expensive birthday parties for the kids? Can't we just have their friends over to our house for cake and ice cream?"

"Where does all our money go?!"

These disagreements can be especially volatile if generational values and beliefs are involved. When a person who grew up in a house where the family lived from paycheck to paycheck marries someone who grew up in a family that freely and extravagantly spent their money regardless of their income, there are bound to be money problems that touch an emotional nerve. Because spending habits are often family based, criticizing the way a spouse spends money is akin to saying "and your mother too."

You can bet that money problems can stress a marriage, but women who know what lies beneath fiscal differences have a real edge against the risk of rising tempers.

Conflict 2: Fighting About Parenting Styles

In your opinion, who's the better parent in your home? When I ask that question to a couple sitting in front of me, I might get a conciliatory accord from the mom and dad acknowledging that they each have positives and negatives. But when I ask who sees themselves as being in charge of the standards by which the children should be raised, almost without exception, the mom gets the nod.

By knowing all the biological, social, and cultural differences between males and females that we've talked about so far, you may now better understand why, if your style of parenting rules your kids, your husband may not quite get why you're in charge of deciding what's right and what's wrong. Remember, he has that need to be right and in control, the need to protect his family, and the need for acknowledgment. He fulfills none of these if he doesn't have a say about how his son or daughter is raised.

In many happy marriages, after both parents agree that the child's safety is paramount, all other parenting decisions are valid. That's the way Karen sees it: "There are many things that Josh does with our four-year-old daughter, Kaitlyn, that I'm tempted to say are bad, crazy, or even irresponsible," she freely admits. "But when I stop myself and think about what he's doing from his point of view, usually it's stuff that's just different from the way I would do it—not necessarily wrong."

To make her point, Karen told me about the day Josh decided to share his favorite pastime with Kaitlyn—fishing. He bought her a pole; they dug for worms and then headed off to a nearby stream. With their day's catch in a sloppy bucket, they headed home and stopped for a few hot dogs on the way. As they walked up to their front door, their laughter abruptly stopped. They saw Karen standing on the steps, hands on her hips. Her daughter's brand-new sneakers were covered with mud, her shirt stunk of dead fish, and the mustard stains around her mouth gave away the fact that her appetite for dinner would be spoiled. Karen looked sternly at both of them and then burst out laughing.

"Would *I* ever let my daughter get that messy?" she asked me. "Probably not. And I certainly had good reason to be angry about the wasted dinner in the oven, but . . . if you could have seen the look of perfect joy on Josh's face, you'd know why I just couldn't take that away from him. Sure he's messy and doesn't always think things through, but he sure loves our daughter."

If Karen had chastised her husband for being irresponsible and acting like a kid himself, how do you think Josh would have reacted? If he's wired like most men, first he would defend himself, then he'd attack to make himself feel more in control of the argument, and finally he would withdraw.

If he and Karen had had this argument over his parenting skills before, it's likely that eventually he would withdraw from his daughter's life as well. With that kind of collateral damage left behind, there are no real winners.

Research confirms over and over again that whether from instinct or social training, moms and dads have different parenting styles. Women are more verbal and nurturing with the kids (typical for the female of the species, who thrives on relationship building and discussion);[7] dads are more action oriented, demanding, and logical[8] (in keeping with the male propensity to express himself through actions and to organize his world logically rather than emotionally). Do these descriptors match the parenting styles in your house?

These differences in parenting styles are quite typical and often immediately apparent. As researchers observed parents playing with their infants, they found that moms often contain a baby's movements by holding his or her legs or hips, while calming the baby down with a soft voice, slow speech, and repeated rhythmic phrases. Fathers, in contrast, often poke their baby; pedal his or her legs; make loud, abrupt noises; and tease and stimulate the infant to higher pitches of excitement.[9] Neither play style is right or wrong; the baby benefits from both.

REMEMBER THIS
A Good Reason to Work It Out

Accepting different parenting styles can keep your marriage secure, and this can have far-reaching benefits for your child. Compared to children living apart from their fathers, children living with two married biological parents are, on average, less likely to be suspended or expelled from school, less likely to engage in delinquent activities, less likely to experience depression and anxiety, and less likely to report externalizing and internalizing behavioral problems.[10]

Differences in parenting styles are a source of conflict, but they are also a great opportunity to work with your man to make your marriage not only happier but also easier. Assuming he doesn't wish your child to be harmed any more than you do, you can agree on guidelines for safety, such as use of a bike helmet and prohibition of bungee cord jumping, then sit back and enjoy the benefits. Let him parent his way, even though it is different from the way you parent. It's good for him to feel that you trust his ability to take care of his children. It's good to give him as much experience at parenting as possible so that he feels more confident and in control. It's good for your marriage to have one less thing to argue about. And it's good for you because it gives you a break.

Conflict 3: Fighting About Leisure Time

When you were first dating your husband, how did you spend your leisure time? In the courting stage, almost all couples spend time in each other's company as frequently as is humanly possible. Even when life was hectic, stolen minutes here and there are coveted and exhilarating.

How do you spend your leisure time now? I know you're probably laughing at the idea that I think you have any leisure time at all. Married life is full of responsibilities that eat up time—house maintenance, laundry, meals, work, kids, and on and on—and suddenly there's this guy living in your house whom you haven't heard laugh in . . . well, you can't remember when.

Because the obligations of married life can suck all the free time out of your day, what few unstructured moments there are become coveted entities that require serious thought about how they will be spent. When your choice includes your spouse, believe me your guy notices and is grateful. For example, in discussions in my office, a thirty-two-year-old client named Jack complimented his wife because she chose him over the gym. He explained, saying,

> Mara is just the best. The other day she was headed out to the gym at the same time that I was getting ready to walk our dog. We both stopped dead in our tracks—we each thought the other was going to be home to watch the kids. There was this sudden silent agreement that whoever spoke first was going to be the one staying home. Then, I couldn't believe it. Mara picked up the baby and called to our four-year-old saying, "Come on guys. We're going for a walk with Daddy and Max." Just like that she was willing to get her exercise by walking with me and the kids. I didn't say anything to her at the time, but really appreciated what she did.

Wow! I was surprised that Jack was so open about the way his wife's decision affected him, but it was a pretty typical example of how choosing to spend leisure time with one's spouse affects the quality of the marriage.

Of course, some disputes over leisure time are a bit more complicated. There are some spouses who totally neglect their families in favor of the golf course, their buddies or girlfriends, or even technology. In fact, what I call "electronic interference" complaints have been creeping into my therapy sessions more and more often lately. And, although similar to the marital conflict over feelings of neglect caused by a spouse who's never home, this one is related to feelings of abandonment caused by a spouse who *is* at home.

This is the problem that bothers Lynn, who offered a response to my Internet question "What habit of your husband annoys you the most?" She wrote,

> I guess his most annoying thing is when he spends time on his computer doing his office e-mail and other work, researching something that interests him, scouring the news media and blogs, and playing games when he could be spending time with me. What annoys me most is that we'll make plans to watch our favorite TV show or go for a walk after dinner and he just blows me off because he's doing something on his laptop. I just don't get him sometimes.

Welcome to the twenty-first century. I firmly believe that the overuse of computers, video games, and other electronic entertainment and communication devices is a new thorn in the side of marital bliss. In fact, at least one study now reports that even cell phone use is linked to higher distress and lower family satisfaction—especially when it causes work to intrude on family time.[11] There's no doubt that as computers, cell phones, Blackberries, and other devices increasingly intrude on our family time, these high-tech conveniences are bound to cause new kinds of martial arguments in the "you never give me your time or attention" category of conflict.

It's not just the latest electronic contraptions that are problematic. Even good old-fashioned television can erode relationships. Italian researchers surveyed over five hundred couples and found that those without bedroom TVs have sex twice as often as television watchers. And the older the couple, the bigger the gap: Once a couple was over fifty, the study found that average sex rates went down from 7 times a month to 1.5 times a month if there was a TV in the bedroom.[12]

The root of this disconnect over how couples use their leisure time—whether it's spent out of the house or with an electronic device—is not really about the amount of time spent apart, but rather about how each partner perceives the priorities of the other. Lynn's not angry that her husband spends so much time on his computer; she's angry that he would rather do that than spend time with her. And on the weekend, when a spouse spends more time on the tennis court, at the club, or with friends at the local diner than he or she does at home, his or her partner feels unimportant and abandoned. That's fuel for some vicious fights.

When potential conflicts arise, your mission, should you choose to accept it, is to find balance and happiness again in the marriage. And, as is often the case, it's the female who, with her more finely developed interpersonal skills, may be better equipped to accept the mission (Now I've gone from war imagery to *Mission Impossible* clichés!). As a wife, you have a chance to take the first positive step and use conflict-resolution strategies (like those in the next section) to negotiate an agreeable solution.

SIX TIPS FOR FIGHTING BETTER

I've come to accept that wherever you find two individuals who share wedding vows, you'll find two individuals who will share arguments. When all the stories are aired and the complaints lodged, the bottom line almost always is simple: He or she should see things the way I do. Given what we know about males and females, and individuals in general, this isn't going to happen anytime soon. You can try to change your husband and get him to do things your way all the time; that is unlikely to work, but even if it did, it would make for a pretty boring life. The chemistry between happily married couples thrives on the fact that you're two unique human beings, and your different points of view and different personalities are what make life full and interesting.

Still, the conflicts that arise out of these differences do disturb the marital peace. To keep the noise down and to keep little tiffs from escalating into drawn-out battles, here are six tips to help you fight better.

Tip 1: Take the Lead

This first tip is a quick and easy one. Would you like to get your husband to do what you want? Tell him what it is! It is so frustrating for men when their wives expect them to know what to do and when to do it. Get away from the "I shouldn't have to tell him" mind-set.

Sharing a Secret

"Ninety-Nine Percent of the Time, We Find a Solution."

When there are big issues worth arguing over, I've learned never to start that discussion when either of us is upset. I'll clam up, refuse to argue, but then wait until a time we're both more at ease and open to honest communication. Then I talk about it, constructively—no accusations, no scolding or nagging—just present the problem and how it affects me, then ask him what we can do to fix it. This puts the problem in a positive light, rather than putting him or me on the defensive. Ninety-nine percent of the time, we find a solution, or one of us will give in for sake of saving the relationship. Personally, I find it much easier to "give in" to his viewpoint when we face the problem together, rather than from opposing, defensive, or aggressive positions.

—Karen, age 25, married 2 years

My coauthor has taken a first step in this direction in the very midst of writing this chapter:

Last week I was flipping through a magazine and found one of those perfume inserts that I usually just throw away. But this one was a really nice blend of what the ad called "oriental and spicy harmony." I gave it to my husband (who is often at a loss around my birthday and Mother's Day for gift ideas) and said, "Isn't this a nice fragrance? I really like it." He replied, "Yeah," never even looking at the ad or catching the name of the perfume. My impulse was to roll my eyes and throw it out, but then I remembered this suggestion about taking the lead. So I saved the ad and will tape it to the mirror just before my next birthday with a note that says, "Buy this for my birthday!" Instead of feeling annoyed at his insensitivity to what I thought was an obvious hint, I'm looking forward to getting exactly what I want.

Yes, you do have to be very direct with a man. Here are some tips that women say work for them (almost) every time:

- Want him to remember your birthday? Remind him. Send him an e-mail. Post a sticky note on the bathroom mirror. Don't sit around hoping he'll remember— that may lead to disappointment. Instead, be proactive to get what you want.

- If ever you're tempted to say, "If you don't know why I'm angry, I'm not going to tell you," stop yourself. It's very likely that he really doesn't know why you're angry, so making him guess is frustrating for everybody. The only way to get your needs met is to speak up.

- Upset because your husband is distracted by the TV when you have something important to say? Don't fume and wait for him to catch on that you need his attention. Go over to the TV during a commercial and ask him if you can turn it off for a second. Then talk fast.

Tip 2: Use Your Superior Communication Skills

Females have the potential to triumph in verbal fights because they are usually better at using words to express their emotions. It's been shown that from elementary school up until high school, girls are able to perform better in the language arts than boys. Remember that men can't as easily access the emotions *and* the language center of the brain at the same time. When they are angry, words will frequently fail them (which is probably why, when they're with other men struggling with the same handicap, they often resort to talking with their fists).

Your superior communication skills are an advantage that can work to your benefit during an argument, if you remember to use them in ways that men can understand.

In the upcoming chapter, we'll look at four lessons about talking with a man that will come in handy during any marital spat. In the meantime, you can increase your chances of having a happy ending in the next argument with your hubby if you remember to allow him to feel that he's being heard.

If you're like so many of the women I counsel, when you talk to other women, you seek ways to find areas of agreement, you reiterate what you heard, you make the speaker feel really important. In other words, you give the speaker the impression that you are listening. Using these same listening skills with your husband will make him feel that you hear what he's struggling to say and are making an attempt to understand him. You already know how to make someone feel heard; you must use that skill on your husband. You may not even know how it is that you do make your friends feel heard; you may never have dissected the steps that lead to your sister's always calling *you* when she breaks up with a boyfriend. Researchers have broken down the elements of being a good listener; here's all you have to do:

1. Take a minute and repeat back what you thought you heard your partner say. "If I understand you correctly, you're saying . . ." and then repeat back exactly what you heard, even if it means using the same words.

2. Make sure your mate is understood by seeking confirmation that you did hear his message: "Is that what you're trying to say?"

3. Allow for clarifications if your partner claims you missed the point. "Okay, explain that part again so I can be clear." Then wait for a response.

4. Don't jump in with "Yes, but . . . ," or "What you need to understand is . . . ," because these give the message that you're only listening to correct. People don't feel heard if they're being corrected. You only want to make sure he knows that you are eager to discover what he's getting at.

5. Make clear that you wish to have a clear understanding of the whole message: "OK, I think I understand now. You're concerned about . . ."

6. Once your listener feels heard, you have an option. You can use that as a break point, and say, "I really appreciate having the whole picture; let me think about it for a while," or you can then move to speak what's on your mind.

REMEMBER THIS
A Weapon of Peace

When I do workshops and lectures, I sometimes show photos of someone's eyes and
ask audience members if they can read any
emotion without seeing the rest of the face. With the
exception of that "come hither" look of desire, men
are just not as capable of reading emotions as women
are. Women are quite good at translating all facial
expressions; they are able to better perceive subtle
changes in emotion and read changes in facial appear-
ance, body language, and tonal inflection. In some circles, this is called "woman's intuition," and it's a
powerful weapon for peace when it's used to figure out
what a man is really thinking and feeling.

The benefits of making this effort to use active listening
will be clear as you begin to realize that you're actually getting
through to him when you argue. When your man feels heard,
he'll be much more open to your point of view.

Tip 3: Consider Both Sides

Getting him to see your point of view is good, but even better for a peaceful household is letting yourself see *his* point of
view also. I'm sure you realize that if there were only one way
to view the situation, you wouldn't be having the argument.
Recognizing the possibility that both of you have a good reason for seeing it the way you do is a solid move toward having
better arguments.

This was the skill that Karen used so well when Josh and Kaitlyn walked up to the house after their fishing trip looking like an ad for laundry detergent. She was able to see past her own anger long enough to consider her husband's point of view. "Although it drives me crazy when he acts like the kid instead of the adult," she admits, "I know that most of the things he does that annoy me are just one way of doing things that doesn't happen to be my way. But none of them are things meant to deliberately hurt me, and that's what I have to remember before I turn it into a big deal."

Smart woman, that Karen. Motive. Motive. Before moving into attack mode, always ask yourself what the other point of view might be: "What's his motive here? Is it his intention to hurt me? To demean me? To ridicule me?" Then answer honestly. Women who tell me they are happy to be married are also usually the ones who realize that although their man may do things differently than they do, he is not cruel or evil in his intent.

Tip 4: Use Soft Start-Ups

Even when you know your husband does not have evil intentions, his actions or words can still hurt. In the heat of an argument, you feel wronged! You've been hurt. How do you respond?

I know that the impulse to react with harsh words can be strong (*You're such a jerk!*), but given what we now know about men and their need to fend off feelings of shame, there's no way a verbal attack is going to get you what you want. This puts your man on the defensive, shuts down his ability to listen objectively, and sparks that competitive need to win—no matter who's right or wrong. Not only that, but researchers show us that if an argument starts with hostility, nine times out of ten it will still be harsh by its conclusion.[13]

The next time you're tempted to lash out with criticism, stop and rethink your opening line: turn it into an "I" statement. This is actually a method I learned when I was training in psychotherapy. To reduce my client's defensiveness, I'd point out my observations, rather than point out his or her faults. Because I was offering my perspective, my statements usually included the pronoun "I" rather than "you." I might say, for instance, "I notice you seem to be upset at the exorbitant cost for my services," rather than "You're pissed at my bill, aren't you!" Using "I" statements helped open up dialogue.

Let me explain why this is so critical for successfully navigating a disagreement. Your husband is preprogrammed by eons of evolutionary male genetics to want to protect you— make you happy. If you make him feel unsuccessful in that quest with verbal criticism that "puts him in his place," you leave him without a constructive way of salvaging his pride.

If instead you open up a dialogue by discussing your sense of unease, he will be more inclined to seek a way to make you feel comfortable. When he hears you say, "I feel lonely when you work so many late hours," he's more likely to consider your point of view. If you continue to avoid attacking his behavior, he'll soon see for himself the reason his actions upset you.

Let's try some soft start-ups. I'll give you a typical "you" statement and then you see if you can design your own noncritical way of addressing the given problem. Use a bookmark or ruler to hide my suggested soft start-up response until you try your own.

Parenting problem: He lets the kids stay up late to watch TV on a school night.

Criticism: "You are so irresponsible. Don't you realize the kids have school tomorrow!?"

Soft start-up: "I feel overwhelmed managing the kids the next day when they don't get a good night's sleep."

Money problem: He buys an expensive new car after nixing your vacation plans because the trip would cost too much money.

Criticism: "All you think about is you! Why are you the only one who gets to spend money around here?"

Soft start-up: "I'm hurt that such an important decision was made without my input."

Leisure-time problem: He wants to skip your nephew's birthday party to run a marathon with his friends.

Criticism: "You always blow off events that involve my family. Can't you show some common courtesy?"

Soft start-up: "Sometimes I feel like I'm low on your priority list."

This strategy works well with the major areas of conflict, but also with the minor annoyances of everyday married life. Here are a few typical scenarios that may sound familiar:

Problem: He leaves his socks on floor.

Criticism: "Don't you ever pick up for yourself!?"

Soft start-up: "I feel like I have to work harder when you leave clothes on the floor" or "When you leave socks around, it makes me feel like you don't care if we have a neat home."

Problem: He interrupts you in the middle of conversation.

Criticism: "You're so rude! Do you think you're the only one in the room that has something important to say?"

Soft start-up: "I feel devalued when you don't let me finish" or "It makes me feel rotten when I feel like you're not listening."

Problem: He wants to have sex when you're feeling distracted.

Criticism: "Is sex all you think about?!"

Soft start-up: "I value our sexual connection, but it's difficult for me to think about sex right now" or "I sometimes feel like your not paying attention to how I feel when you bring up sex."

You can see how using a more gentle approach short-circuits harshness and opens up your man to dialogue. That alone is a great way to fight better.

Tip 5: Use Your Feminine Strengths

Women have a naturally strong ability to soothe their children, and some women are clever enough to use that same nurturing skill with their husbands to reduce household tensions. When her husband is upset, fifty-four-year-old Jacklyn will reach out and touch him. Without even knowing that this gesture helps reduce his level of stress hormones, emotional arousal, blood pressure, and stomach acid, she has intuitively learned over their twenty-five-year marriage that her touch can ease a bad mood, especially the kind that with little provocation can quickly turn into an argument.

"When Marc starts picking on silly things, like the way I leave my shoes by the front door," says Jacklyn, "I know he's

just in a bad mood and looking to find an outlet (like by arguing with me). When that happens, I've learned that I can
calm his nerves by making a physical gesture of affection,
maybe like giving him a hug, squeezing his upper arm, or sitting on his lap. It's amazing how well this works!"

Sure, it would be nice if your husband would do the same
thing for you once in a while, but being female, you're the one
blessed with this exquisite ability to tame the beast with just
a touch. You are the one attuned to the fact that he's upset
emotionally—he may not recognize that feeling for himself
(*I'm fine!*). This ability to read social cues is probably encouraged more in young females than in males, but there's evidence that it's also inborn. Remember that in Chapter One
we discussed studies in which infant girls—but not boys—
responded to the distress of other infants.

It's a gift—a gift that enables you to read the feelings and
thoughts of others, detect emotional subtleties, and respond
in appropriate ways. It's not always a "Poor baby!" a guy is
looking for—this can sound like an attempt to diminish his
manhood. But he is frequently open to being touched and
held when he's upset or sad. If you use your skills when your
guy is upset, angry, and looking for a fight, you will often be
able to calm him down and avoid the fight entirely—or at
least to fight better.

Tip 6: Pile on the Compliments

Want to argue less? Compliment more. It really is as simple as
that. Saying good things about your guy when talking to him
(or about him) colors the way you see him in your heart.
Putting him down highlights his weaknesses and paints him

REMEMBER THIS
Who's the Stubborn One in Your House?

Many women tell me that they've married a man who will never admit that he's wrong, but statistics suggest that, on average, it may be the woman who digs in her heels—at least that's how the men see it. One study of 457 couples found that wives perceived themselves as giving in about as often as their husbands, but husbands saw themselves giving in five times as often as their wives![14]

as a louse. Heck, of all the people in the world who might give your husband a daily boost, you should be the one he can count on.

Besides just being a nice thing to do, complimenting your spouse can be a real marriage saver. Researchers have found that a strong predictor of marital success is the ratio of positive to negative interactions between spouses. In successful marriages, the positive interactions outnumber the negative five to one.[15] How does this compare to the ratio of positive to negative interactions you've had with your husband today?

There are plenty of ways to boost this number: Positive interactions include expressing kind words, paying attention, providing a pleasant experience, making conciliatory gestures, and expressing compliments. And you can cut back on negative behaviors, which include complaining, criticizing, mocking, insulting, whining, communicating contempt, or ignoring him.[16]

Although this makes sense, you may wonder if this strategy will have you doing all the positive stuff while your husband continues to complain and criticize. Not to worry. Keeping the ratio high on the positive side has the amazing capacity to turn even a cold, isolated spouse around very quickly.

This tactic worked well for Eliana, a recent medical school graduate who had problems adjusting to life with her lawyer husband, Graham. She worked four half days a week, and jumped right into caring for her two children from the minute her feet hit the welcome mat.

After Graham's long day, though, he came home with a cursory "hello," then disappeared into the basement to do . . . well, actually she wasn't sure what he did . . . on his cell phone. She was smart enough to know that she would be inviting a long, drawn-out fight if she attacked his skewed priorities and insisted that he give her more attention. "Been there, done that." So I suggested that she try the positive approach.

Eliana beamed when she came into my office two weeks later. "Bingo! It worked. We haven't felt this connected in years!"

"Really?" I asked (just a little surprised, given Eliana's degree of discontent).

> I can't believe I didn't see the reason why Graham was hooked on his cell phone. He's the kind of guy who worries that he'll miss something important at the office if he doesn't check his voicemail every hour. He's invested a lot of time in his work, and he is up for partner in the next few months. Usually he's an amazingly confident man, but part of his

withdrawal from the family had to do with a growing insecurity with whether he'd measure up to the
high standards he had for himself. All I had to do
was make him feel good about himself with me. It
really was easy. I focused on his strengths. I complimented and praised him over the smallest accomplishments at home. You'd think I'd told him he was
just nominated as the attorney general! It wasn't
long before he was giving me more attention and
focusing less on his work at the office. I never would
have won this disagreement by fighting about it.
This was a much better approach.

Yes. Finding good things about your spouse and pointing
them out builds your relationship and cuts down on arguments. If you have children, you know that you can mold their
behavior better by complimenting the good things than by
scolding the bad. And many very happy wives know that the
same tactic works with husbands.

Stroke, don't poke. If every time your husband walks in
the door he knows he'll hear something kind and nice, he's
bound to start returning the attitude back toward you. When
that happens (and it will), yours is going to be a very happy
marriage.

PATCHING IT UP WHEN
THE ARGUMENT IS OVER

The goal is not to stop disagreements in your marriage—you'll
never be able to do that. But you can learn to fight better
about those disagreements. And when the fight is over, you
can learn to make up better, too. In fact, knowing how to

REMEMBER THIS
Sometimes You Have to
Agree to Disagree

Most of your disagreements (researchers say a whopping 69 percent of them) are never going to be resolved.[17] And there's a growing body of research that suggests there is no such thing as a truly and totally compatible couple.[18] So starting today, ease your grip on the mistaken notion that happy couples work out all their problems—they don't. Instead, do less fighting by recognizing the issues that the two of you will never agree on. Then, agree to disagree. So much easier.

make up after a fight is a vital strategy for building a happy marriage. In a study of newlyweds, the couples that could not patch things up after a fight had a rate of divorce in excess of 90 percent. But when couples were successful at making up, the odds of divorce dropped to a mere 16 percent.[19] Obviously this is a skill worth working on.

Patching things up can take many forms, from bringing a cup of tea to expressing an "aw shucks," but in all cases its success depends on three factors: a heartfelt desire to reconnect, an openness on the part of the person who's receiving the olive branch, and a calm mental state when offering forgiveness. Often couples don't realize that when the alarm centers of the brain get activated, it's hard to let go of bad feelings. Sometimes it can take up to a half hour or longer for the arousal system to wind down. Then, and only then, should the patch-up take place.

Now here is one place in the fight arena where men have the advantage. They are usually better able to walk away and start anew as if nothing happened. But making up is sometimes especially difficult for women, for three very good reasons:

1. Women's higher levels of estrogen cause them to feel the hurt of an argument more deeply than men do. This is because estrogen activates a larger field of neurons in females in an upsetting situation, causing them to experience the stress more intensely.[20] Your higher level of intense emotion during a fight cuts to your core. You can literally feel your heart ache.

Men, in contrast, fight hard and then it's done. Their feelings of anger are less likely to bleed into sorrow, rejection, or depression.

2. Women have more memory of each detail of the fight long after it's over. It's quite common for a woman, in the middle of an argument, to say something like "Well, you're the one who started this by giving my brother a hard time when he visited the house three Christmases ago!" Suddenly your husband's gears will grind to a halt, and he'll deny any recollection of this past event. And now you have a whole new topic to fight over. But he really doesn't remember. In a research study, men did not show increased brain blood flow in the memory center (the hippocampus) when negative emotions were triggered,[21] suggesting a diminished ability to recall or process disturbing events. But soon after the woman's amygdala gets activated, her hippocampus becomes flooded with increased blood flow, and thus a woman is much more likely to recall incidents that aroused negative emotions.

Other research shows that a female's higher estrogen level also contributes to her ability to remember stressful events more clearly than a male. Estrogen prolongs the amount of time that the adrenal gland secretes the stress hormone cortisol—a natural memory booster.[22]

3. Not only are you better able to remember the details of a stressful situation, unlike males who are able to forget what happened and move on, you're programmed to go over and over that situation in your mind. The female sex hormone progesterone blocks the normal ability of the stress hormone system to turn itself off, making females biologically prone to internally amplifying their negative life experiences. They are likely to ruminate over negative thoughts and feelings far longer than their male partner.[23]

Given that you feel the hurt more deeply, remember the painful details more clearly, and spend more time going over and over the hurt you feel, it's no wonder you're less willing to forgive and forget. In fact, you probably find it infuriating when your man ends an argument by saying, "Wanna go get some pizza?" He's ready to move on. You're not.

But it's important that you do. Personally, you might want to punish your husband for his cruel remark by freezing him out of your life for a week or so. But this is a time you should ask yourself if doing this will bring you closer to your goal of having a happy marriage. Happy wives are committed to staying married to their guy for the long haul, so they're willing to make their point and move on. Besides, all that negative energy takes a lot of work, and we're looking for ways for you to do less and still be happy.

The Do Less Lesson

Even the most delightfully happy women butt heads with their husbands every once in a while. You can't prevent all conflict, but rather than fear it, you can keep it from escalating into all-out war. In fact, by honing your abilities to clarify your husband's needs, direct attention to shared values, and lovingly show him how to reduce tensions, you can use disagreements as a way to understand each other. You'll fight less, you'll fight better, and you'll still have a chance to express yourself and get your needs met.

4

Talk Less

If you struggle to understand what seems to be a communication deficit in your marriage, this chapter offers you an opportunity to increase the joy in your household and in your heart by playing to your strength: your exceptionally advanced ability to communicate. However, this opportunity requires that you learn to speak the language of men, which I call *Man-ese*. It's a quick and direct kind of interaction that will help you get what you need and want out of your guy and at the same time will help him learn how to listen and respond when you talk.

THE EXTREME MALE BRAIN

Men are commonly labeled poor communicators. Yet as world leaders in business, commerce, and politics, these very same men do manage to get the job done. How is that possible if they use the same communication skills that cause their wives to complain, "He never listens"?

It's possible because males use kinds of communication skills that have proven very effective in the workplace but that are often disastrous in personal relationships. This difference makes it appear that men and women speak entirely different languages.

Men tend to be very objective in their conversations. They talk about factual stuff like global politics, finances, poker, fishing, and of course sports—all for the purpose of making a definable point as they analyze opponents, strategies, goals, and results. If they have a point to make, they talk only until they've made the point. Good. Done. They've said what they had to say. If they don't have a point to make, they don't talk.

 **REMEMBER THIS**
It's Not Our Strong Suit

I have a good friend, Mark. He always gives me a hard time about the fact that I write books. (For guys, ribbing is a form of bonding and drawing closer.) "I don't see how you can write a whole book on being a good husband," he says. "Just teach men to say three sentences: Yes, Dear. You're right, Dear. I'm sorry, Dear." According to Mark, my last book should have been just eight words long. The difficulty with this helpful piece of advice is that women don't really want men to utter these empty phrases. Women want husbands who tune in to them, understand them, and seek a mutually positive interaction. But the problem with many men is that even if they feel the same way, they often have a tough time saying it. Personal verbal communication is not their strong point—but it is yours.

Women, in contrast, tend to be subjective talkers. Their conversations are very often about feelings and about the whole picture of daily events, including descriptions of surrounding details that wander far from the main point, but add rich texture to the story. Sometimes they talk about what men call "nothing." But this kind of talk has a real purpose to women. They talk to build relationships, bond, get to know another person, seek understanding, and offer empathy. That's what having a directionless chat is really all about.

Chatting soothes women's souls, but it drives men crazy. Most women find a man's inability to have a nice conversation without getting fidgety, interrupting, or zoning out horribly frustrating. So what's a couple to do?

Happy couples recognize and accept the differences between male and female communication styles. The wives, especially, let go of the idea that "he could be a better communicator if he wanted to." Certain biological differences suggest that he can't. In fact, one body of research points to the possibility that there may very well be a connection between the way some men struggle with interpersonal communication and the fact that the neurological disorder of autism is four times more likely to affect boys than girls.[1]

Let's take a closer look at the common traits of autism, and you'll see how incredibly male they sound. A child who has autism will often stare into some space that seems all his own, and it is hard to get his attention. Such a child will often focus intently on one object or thought, and block out other distractions. Usually, he is drawn toward inanimate objects rather than conversations between people. The autistic child often seems to be in his own little world; he is often happiest when left alone and can become irritable or agitated if you try to redirect him. Understanding facial cues or tone of voice is hard for the autistic child, and he has difficulties tuning into the feelings of others. Does any of this sound like your husband? If so, the cause of his communication blocks could be biological.

Although no one genetic mechanism has been identified as the root of autism, an interesting theory has been proposed by Dr. Simon Baron-Cohen of Cambridge University, which gives a reasonable biological explanation and a potential link between the disorder and the male brain. Baron-Cohen believes that prenatal levels of the male hormone testosterone may determine whether an individual has a predominantly "male brain" or "female brain." He says the male brain is characterized by a tendency to systematize (identify how things work), whereas the female brain is characterized by a tendency to empathize (identify and relate to the feelings of others). Baron-Cohen believes that individuals with autism have an "extreme male brain."[2] So if you have an image of a man who sits staring at his computer screen blocking you out, staring dumbly into your face when you talk about your feelings, and giving the distinct impression that his own desire to be left in peace trumps any needs you have at the moment, you have a good idea of why I draw parallels between autism and male behavior. And you'll also appreciate why encouragement, rather than badgering, will help move this man into a more engaging style of human interaction.

THE DIFFERENCE BETWEEN
TALK AND COMMUNICATION

When I read articles about improving relationships, the words "talk" and "communicate" are frequently used synonymously. But they are not the same. Men may not talk as much as women do, but they do communicate very well—if you're alert to their nonverbal messages.

It's What He Does, Not What He Says

Females, with their strong and numerous connectors between the right and left brain hemispheres, are easily able to access their emotions from the right brain and put them into words with the left brain. But without as many connectors between the brain hemispheres, males can find it tough to be as emotionally expressive. Although they certainly do feel emotions deeply and can be verbally expressive, they can't readily do both at the same time.

But that doesn't mean they don't communicate their feelings. As Elizabeth Barrett Browning so eloquently put it: "How do I love thee? Let me count the ways." Pay attention, and you may be able to count the many ways your husband is reaching out to you emotionally, without saying a word.

We know that many men prefer to let their actions do their talking, especially (as we explored in Chapter One) when it comes to saying "I love you" or "I'm sorry." In fact, often a guy learns from his dad that love is expressed by doing things together ("Come on son, let's throw the ball around") rather than by proclaiming affection with words.

If your man isn't free with declarations of love, you might recognize the sentiment when he says, "Let's go play tennis." Or you might see it when he demonstrates his commitment to you with action by protecting you when he drops you off at a store entrance while he then parks the car in the rain, by taking responsibility for getting the bills paid on time, by toiling to get a promotion at work, by *doing* over and over again. Count the ways.

A man's inability to say thank you when his wife feels he should is another sensitive issue in many marriages. Let's say you work hard preparing a special meal that he loves. You're bound to feel hurt if he gulps it down greedily without ever verbally expressing his appreciation. That's when you have to remember to look (rather than listen) for emotional communication. True, he didn't use words to say thanks, but he clearly conveyed the message by devouring the dish and asking for seconds. You wanted to please him, and you obviously did! Oh come on, you're saying. He can't say thank you? Of course he can, but some men are programmed to let their actions speak louder than their words.

And then there's the way men communicate that they're in the mood. In movies and in romance novels, the lover stares into the leading lady's eyes while gently brushing a stray hair into place and says, "Darling, you look beautiful. I want to hold you in my arms and make passionate love to you right now." But your man is more likely to give you a wink and a nod toward the bedroom. How unromantic! But to him life isn't the movies; it is more natural and realistic for him to communicate his desire without a word.

Happy is the woman who knows that relating to a man realistically means acknowledging that although he expresses himself differently than she does, his feelings are no less meaningful, real, or intense.

Body Signs

Men also communicate through their nonverbal body language. This is another way for them to "talk" through their actions—and one more opportunity for you to help your husband open up in a way that's comfortable for him.

Guyness Quotient Quiz

How Would Your Guy Answer?

Okay, so you have decided that you truly love a woman and want to spend the rest of your life with her—sharing the joys and the sorrows, the triumphs and the tragedies, and all the adventures and opportunities that the world has to offer, come what may. How do you tell her?

a. You take her to a nice restaurant and tell her after dinner.

b. You take her for a walk on a moonlit beach; you say her name, and when she turns to you, with the sea breeze blowing her hair and the stars in her eyes, you tell her.

c. Tell her what?

Let's say, for example, that a husband comes home from work looking upset. His shoulders are hunched; his face muscles are tensed, his jaw clenched. His wife asks with a sympathetic tone, "How was your day, honey?" And he says, "All right." Right then and there this wife has a choice to make.

In the home that is filled with tension due to a communication disconnect, the wife's sympathy turns to anger; she feels hurt and excluded.

"It's obvious that things are *not* all right. Why do you say that?" she demands. "Why can't you talk to me?"

She immediately assumes that her husband's short and untrue response means that he doesn't care about her or trust her enough to talk about important things. She is so hungry for the words, which she relies on to build connections, that she misinterprets his method of communication.

REMEMBER THIS
"But He Used to Talk"

Many women will tell me that they didn't see their man as silent at all when they were dating. In fact, they will describe hours and hours of deep conversations into the night. It's probably true. During the dating phase, the connection hormones that spark that lovin' feeling—dopamine and norepinephrine—are at their highest levels, and contribute to a physical sensation of being high. Like an individual who is under the influence of drugs, a lover in such a state can be more talkative, more focused on the interests of others, and an altogether great chatting companion. In other words, your recollections of a man who was keen to talk about his feelings were *not* imaginary. One take-home lesson from this is that new situations help stimulate conversation; introducing novel and exciting experiences into the relationship can get words rolling off his tongue, at least for a little while!

But in the home down the street, where the wife knows the secret of Man-ese communication, the outcome of this conversation starter is quite different. This woman knows that her husband's words say, "All right," but that his body language tells the real story. "Listening" to his body language, she hears him loud and clear. She knows that he's held himself up straight all day and that as he crossed the threshold of his home, his shoulders slumped. Because he trusts her to understand his language, he allows his body to show his fatigue and upset. Later in the evening, after he's had time to process his feelings, it's very likely that this "uncommunicative" husband will fill in the details for his wife. But to get him to that point, she will have to patiently allow him to talk less and communicate more.

The Strong and Silent Type

Some men are so well trained to hide their feelings that they don't give them away even with their body language. They bear their problems alone, and no one in the family has any idea of what's really going on in their emotional life. We have all heard news reports of men going berserk and then doing awful things like holding a loved one hostage, jumping off a bridge, or even killing family members. When the reporter interviews family and friends, they all say, "I had no idea that anything was wrong."

Some men hide their feelings from the rest of the world. That's just the way some men are, and nagging, pleading, and even being understanding and patient will not get them to open up. In fact, such an approach usually has the exact opposite effect; men typically become silent in response to demands for communication they cannot fulfill. For these men, sometimes just being by their side is enough to help them feel more at ease.

TALK LESS STRATEGY

"My husband doesn't talk with me. He never listens, rarely tells me what's on his mind, and simply can't enjoy hanging out and talking."

The problem is common. Typically, the recommended solution involves finding ways to get him to talk. I'm sure you've

REMEMBER THIS
It's Not Always the Guy

Some of my clients don't fit the stereo-
type. Sometimes when I talk about the
need to open up verbally, I see the hus-
band turn to his wife and say, "That's her!" Interestingly, I find that when a woman is the silent type,
then her husband is usually the one who looks for
verbal reassurances, is more attuned to feelings, and
enjoys a more emotionally based relationship. It's
often true that opposites attract.

seen the magazine articles and books that offer tips on how to
get your man to open up, express himself, verbalize his feelings. Sure you can try these things, but it's going to take a
whole lot of work, and despite your best efforts and his willingness to try, I doubt you will have long-term success.

Because of their biological hardwiring and upbringing,
most men will never communicate like women. They will not
listen without interrupting. They will not talk without having a point to make. They will not listen to the details of a
problem without butting in to offer a solution. They will not
enjoy chatting just to pass the time, and they will never be
able to spend the evening talking with their wives about what
they call "nothing."

But that doesn't mean they won't express themselves
through words at all or that there aren't effective tactics that
can help them better understand you. Try the following five
communication strategies. You'll notice that each one is prob-

ably quicker and easier than anything you've tried up to now. And, after all, that's the point—to find more happiness by doing less.

Here are five easy steps to better communication with any guy:

1. Put the point up front.

2. Use fewer words.

3. Talk in his language.

4. Give him time to respond.

5. Watch your timing.

Put the Point up Front

The average male attention span is five minutes; the average female attention span is fifteen minutes.[3] See the problem? Your girlfriends can stay with the story while you build the surrounding details and lead up to the point, but a guy has clocked out before you're anywhere near the point. That's the primary reason they really are guilty of "not listening." They listen for just so long and then mentally move on to something else. This masculine trait begs for women to get to the point faster. Please!

Marilyn's story of a very typical, true-life conversation with a member of the male species illustrates his eagerness for "just the facts, ma'am":

> When my husband came home from work and asked, "What's new?" I started to tell him this little tidbit about our dog, Shana. I began to give some background about how Shana followed me down the stairs into the basement earlier in the day, but

then half-way into the second sentence of the story, he walked into the next room and came back with the mail so he could sort through it (probably thinking that this was going to be a long story of no interest to him). Ya gotta love a guy who can multitask while patiently waiting for me to get to the point. The far-off look told me that I'd better cut to the chase quickly.

There have been times when I tried to add the details of complexity that color all aspects of a story, set up the situation and describe the context before giving the headline. I believe that the big picture

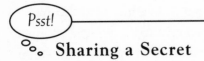

Sharing a Secret

"This Is a Man Who Likes to Get Right to the Point!"

It's a good thing I understand the way my husband communicates or I'd find his curt responses to my e-mails really annoying. The other day I sent him a detailed message explaining how he might be able to get into a Web site that for some unknown reason was blocked on his computer. I also added a note asking what he would like for dinner and then I signed off with words of love. He wrote back: "tried. denied. spaghetti." This is a man who likes to get right to the point!

—Trish, age 46, married 15 years

helps one better understand the point. But when I do that, my husband has been known to walk out, light the grill, come back in, get the dog's leash, let her out in the yard, come back in—always stopping to hear if I'd yet gotten to the point. I'm learning that telling a long, detailed story when he first arrives home from work can be painful for both of us.

So I jumped to the end of the story: "I think Shana is sick." Like magic, I had his full attention!

It is quite predictable that a man, whose mind is still back at work, will make a bad listener to a long story. In some instances, the lack of attention is due to the male's inability to focus in on more than one thing at a time, so if he's still thinking about work or reading the paper or putting a new fishing reel on his pole, he's not going to be listening your story. Other times, due to his male propensity for focused, linear thinking, he is listening only for the bottom line. Men tend to cut right through muddying details to get to the bones of a situation.

In Marilyn's case, she was setting up the scene that would eventually support the key point about the dog's health, but her husband couldn't stand the wait. Her evening was, I'm sure, much happier for both of them because she was smart enough to jump to the punch line and then fill in the details.

Next time you see your husband's mind start to wander while you're talking to him, move directly to the point of your story. I honestly believe that this small change in your communication style, all by itself, has the power to drastically improve your relationship with your husband, making you both oh so much happier.

Use Fewer Words

Think back to the last time you were at a meeting (whether corporate or PTO) or simply with a group of people. It's likely there was one person who loved to talk, loved to hear the sound of his or her own voice. You may have wanted to pay attention and learn something from this person, but probably the point being made (if there was one) got lost in the drone of the details that went on and on and on.

Then someone who had been silent up to then interjected with a softly spoken yet carefully considered and concise point of view. Suddenly, everyone in the room woke up and paid attention. There's no doubt that people who speak less often and use fewer words are more closely listened to. That's how your husband is wired to communicate. Wives who work with, rather than against, this innate need for controlled sound bites feel confident that they're being listened to.

For example, when thirty-three-year-old Fariba wants her husband of seven years to pick up their son from soccer practice, she has learned to say, "Please pick up Alex from soccer at ten-thirty." Period. She then stops talking, knowing that if he wants to know why or needs more information, he'll ask.

"This works so much better than when I used to give him my reasons and the details," she says. "There was a time when I might deliver that same message by saying something like, 'I made a doctor appointment at ten for myself thinking that soccer practice would end at eleven-thirty as it usually does, and then I'd be there in plenty of time to pick up Alex, but this week the coach is ending the practice early and now I won't be able to get there in time. Can you pick him up at ten-thirty?'"

This kind of background information would be easily understood by Fariba's girlfriends, but most men tend to tune out the "chatter." Cutting to the point is so much easier for both of you!

Actually, this is merely a variation of the "put the point up front" strategy—to the extreme. State the point and then stop. This is a real time saver. It gives you lots of extra time for yourself, and you can feel more secure that he's hearing a much higher percentage of what you are saying.

Psst!

Sharing a Secret

"I Can't Just Send Out Vibes"

As a woman, I intuitively know who needs what in my home—my husband's upset about something at work and needs to be alone, the kids are tired and need early bed, my teen daughter needs to talk about something. Often I want someone to know these things about me, but men are for the most part clueless in this department. I realized that my husband really does want to share my hardships, and help make my life easier—but I have to wave a giant flashing sign in his face to let him know (i.e., communicate clearly; I can't just send out vibes). Realizing his nature, instead of fighting over misunderstandings, has been very positive for our marriage.

—Franny, 37, married 15 years

Talk in His Language

Men have a hard time understanding women's language—
it's full of imagery, details, implied meanings, subtle inferences,
tone modulations, and even facial cues. For most guys, language is far simpler. Men naturally pay attention to the content, not the emotion behind it. They use words literally and
say what they mean outright. No hidden messages, no subtle
anything.

That's what Bob, husband to twenty-eight-year-old Lauren,
does. "Last week I came inside after working in the garden all
afternoon," Lauren told me. "I was hoping to get Bob to give
me a backrub (he knows my back will hurt after that kind of
bending-over work). When we were first married, I probably
would have moaned for a while trying to give him the hint—
and ended up very disappointed. Now I know better. I found
him reading the newspaper on the couch, sat down next to
him, and simply said, 'Be my savior and use those strong hands
to knead the muscles in my back.' Easy as that, I got what I
needed from him."

Lauren no longer ends up disappointed as she gobbles down
aspirins for her back pain, because she's learned to be direct
and ask for what she wants. She also has learned to play to her
husband's desire to protect her and be her hero. Smart move,
Lauren.

Many other women I've sat with in my practice honestly
believe that "If my husband loved me, he'd figure out what I
need." If you insist on having him guess at what you want,
you'll have to put a tremendous amount of energy into making that happen. And still there's a good chance it won't. Men
hear the facts ("My back hurts"), but they don't hear the
request for action ("Please spend a few minutes rubbing my

back"), nor do they discern the emotional content behind the words ("Giving me a massage is a powerful way for you to let me know you care about me").

A far easier way to get what you want from a man is to ask for it, using short, simple sentences that put the request up front. Be like Lauren: Be direct, use action words and the active voice. Here's what I mean:

Option 1: I've had a really long day. The kids had a hectic schedule, the phone never stopped ringing, I had a hundred errands to run after work, and I got home really late. I just don't have the energy to cook a meal. (Wait, wait, *wait* for him to suggest take-out.)

Option 2: I'm bringing home take-out for dinner. See you at six.

Option 1: My boss was in an awful mood today, so he it took it out on me. He gave me more work to do than can possibly be done by one person. He was so nasty, too. When I told him I was going to take a lunch break, he barked out something about wasting more company time. It was just terrible the way he spoke to me. (Wait, wait, *wait* for him to reach out and hold you.)

Option 2: Can you give me a hug? I've had a terrible day.

In these examples, can you see the advantages of taking the second option? It's simple. Believe me, as a man, I know that your husband will appreciate the direct approach. It's so difficult for us to try to figure out what you want unless you tell us. And, very important, this style of communicating makes things much easier for you.

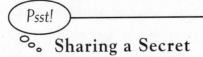

Sharing a Secret

"It Was Difficult Asking Directly"

*On my way home from work I was cranky and
wanted to exercise. I had to stop by the store and
prepare dinner. I was feeling resentful because
I wanted to go for a run. Instead of being crabby
when I got home, I simply told my husband I needed
to go running. I gave him the groceries. And told him
I would like him to cook dinner. He said, "Sure."
I got my run and came home and dinner was ready!
It worked. I wasn't cranky anymore and he con-
tributed. It was difficult asking directly when I was
inclined to whine, be critical (why do I have to do
everything?), and resent not running. Asking for
what you need, and giving your partner time to give
it to you, works. Sometimes.*

—Noel, 39, married 9 years

Give Him Time to Respond

Ever notice that blank look you get from your husband when
you finish talking and wait for his response? Every woman in
the world has seen it—his eyes stare wide-eyed and straight
ahead, his face remains expressionless, his mouth sits slightly
ajar; he looks like he wants to say something, but nothing
comes out. You may have caught him napping while you were
talking, and now he's buying time with his blank stare, hoping to recollect some thread of the conversation—but it's also
possible that he's thinking of what he wants to say.

The lack of strong connection in the corpus callosum that we talked about earlier makes it difficult for a man to access and verbalize his emotions spontaneously. He's not at all stupid, but he does take longer to process important news. You've probably noticed that after he rather abruptly drops a conversation that you thought was important, he'll come back an hour or two later and pick up the subject again. This certainly adds another level of complexity to tapping the silent male mind.

Some women know just how to handle this. They know they'll lose an opportunity to communicate (and keep the peace) if they jump in saying, "Well, aren't you going to say something?" That would shift the focus away from the topic of conversation and on to his inadequacies as a talking companion.

Instead, when they see that stare, they give their guy the benefit of the doubt. They assume he was listening and encourage him to think about what they've said and to come back later with his thoughts on the subject. These women have very happy husbands who know they're blessed.

Watch Your Timing

Your efforts to use Man-ese to better communicate with your husband will fall apart if you ignore this critical piece of advice. Timing is everything. Knowing your man's nature, you know if he is the type who focuses intently on one thing at a time—many men are like that. This one thing may be his career, a big meeting, or a new project that absorbs all his mental energy and attention and makes it difficult for him to break his focus and engage in a conversation. So he ignores his wife, zones out, leaves the room. Here's where she has one of those opportunities to use Man-ese to get what she wants.

Understanding his method of communicating, she knows that his silence says he's preoccupied, he's processing something important, he's trying to figure out his emotions. He can't talk with all that going on. But he is communicating nonverbally that he is temporarily withdrawing from social chit-chat in order to concentrate on something important to him. That's saying a lot to the wife who is paying attention.

As I type this, my wife has begun to tell me a story about something she just heard on the news. Problem is, I'm typing, so I grunt and nod . . . and have no idea what she's talking about. Now she has just left the room without getting any response from me to her story. Susan (who I'd like to think is a happily married woman) knows not to be offended or to feel unloved by my inability to engage in that conversation. She knows it's not an intentional snub, and she'll probably try the story again later at dinner when I'm not distracted.

But I'm sure that in other homes, this same scenario has caused many arguments. It's probably hard for some wives to understand how men can be so oblivious to what they're saying. After all, women can follow a man's conversation while at the same time making dinner, checking their e-mail, and preparing a shopping list. So of course they assume that their husband can divide his attention between the solitary steak on the barbecue grill and a simple conversation. Again: It's very likely that he can't.

Wives who understand this male need to tune out all distractions save themselves much time, effort, and frustration. They know that if they persist in talking to a man who is otherwise busy, they'll probably have to repeat the entire story at another time anyway because he's unlikely to remember and will no doubt fall back on the famous male line, "You never told me that." Make life easier on yourself; if you have something important to share, choose the time wisely.

WHAT ABOUT MY NEED TO TALK?

At this point, I imagine you might be thinking to yourself: If the secret to better communication in a marriage is to speak less and speak less often, where does that leave me when I need to talk? Do I have to forget about ever having meaningful conversations?

If you are the type of woman who truly enjoys all the exciting peaks and mellow valleys, meandering streams and broad horizons of a good talk, I am not suggesting that you can't still employ your style of communicating. It is a valuable part of who you are, and it should not be ignored, either by you or your husband.

(*Psst!*)

°°° Sharing a Secret

"Keep It Short"

After over 17 years of marriage, I have learned to speak "Man." Garrulous incessant chatter is tuned out in favor of visual stimuli (e.g., ESPN). Keep it short, relative, and specific. Also, part of mastering this male language is timing—never discuss weekend plans with two minutes to go in the half with the Eagles down by 3.

—Susan, 42, married 18 years

Certainly, you can have these kinds of talks with your friends any time you want. Some women enjoy talking to their girlfriends either on the phone or over coffee, and appreciate bonding through the power of talking and listening without editing or judgment. Many women who spend time "just talking" with close girlfriends report better connections with their husbands. But understandably, many women also want to have the chance to have that same kind of discussion with their men.

It can be done, but you may need to show him how to be a better communicator:

1. *Remove environmental distractions.* Take your husband into a room that doesn't have a television set or computer (or a wall sconce that's coming slightly loose and needs to be screwed into place with just one itty-bitty screw— hold on, I'll be right back!). This will help keep him focused on you.

2. *Serve up some food.* Sometimes munching helps a man reduce the level of distracting stimuli and makes him more able to kick back and hear you.

3. *Help your hubby understand what your expectations are.* If you just want to talk, tell him, "I feel like sharing some of my thoughts and feelings with you. I'm not looking for a solution or anything; I'd just like to talk." Once he feels that the pressure's off, he can relax and just enjoy spending time with you.

4. *Go for a walk.* Physical activities like walking or working out side-by-side on stationary bicycles can channel your

husband's passion for action and help him stay tuned in to your words.

5. *Give him listening tools. The Secrets of Happily Married Men* is written to give men the tools they need to be great husbands. Chapter Seven in that book is called "Learn to Listen," and it gives men specific guidelines about what their wives need to feel heard, such as "stand still," "make eye contact," and "turn off the TV." If he doesn't have a copy of the book, consider referring him to it if he's still struggling with being a good listener. When men know what they're supposed to do, they're more likely to feel competent and more open to change.

The Do Less Lesson

It's a real time saver to get what you need from a conversation the first time around by speaking in Man-ese, rather than saying the same thing over and over again in language your husband doesn't understand. Instead of pleading and begging him to listen or to do something (and then finally exploding because he responds with, "You never asked me to do that!"), try being short, concise, and direct. With this style of communication, you can say it once, knowing that the message was delivered and received in a language he understands.

5

Have Lots of Sex

H ave you heard the one about the "husband store"? It's a
joke that's been forwarded around by e-mail and goes
like this:

> In the Husband Store, women progress up each floor
> looking for the right man to marry. On the first
> floor, they can find men with jobs; on the next floor,
> there are men with jobs and who are good looking.
> By the time the women are on the fifth floor, they
> can get themselves romantic, handsome men who
> are good with kids, have jobs, and help with house-
> work. As women go up one further floor, they are
> confronted with a sign telling them, "You are cus-
> tomer number 1,326,899. There are no husbands
> here. This floor exists to prove that women are
> impossible to please. Thanks for shopping with us."

I don't retell this joke to make any negative statements
about the nature of women. I pass it on as we open this

chapter on sex because it has a second part that's instructive about the nature of men. The sequel goes something like this:

> In the Wife Store, where men can find the right woman to marry, the first floor has wives who are attractive. The second floor has wives who are attractive and love sex.
>
> The third through sixth floors have never been visited.

As a guy, I find this funny. And as a researcher, I concur with the adage that all humor has a grain of truth. Most men like sex (defined in his mind as intercourse), and most married men like sex with their wives. In fact, they *love* sex with their wives.

Let me explain this last statement before I dedicate the rest of the chapter to the wheres, whats, and hows of having a great sex life. When I say guys love having sex with their wives, I don't mean "love" like the passion inspired by a great fillet mignon in mushroom peppercorn sauce, or by the third movement of their favorite Beethoven symphony. I mean "love" like a deep sense of personal and interpersonal satisfaction that solidifies their connection with their wives and makes them feel that in some small corner of a chaotic world, all is right.

For your man, having sex makes him feel loved *and* makes him love you. It is a vitally important part of his marriage, and for many men it is the glue that makes the marriage stick.

Here is the point where many women have interrupted my theory about sex and marriage (even though I'm just getting going) to insist, "You say this because you're a man."

Yes! That's my point. Because I am a married man who makes a living talking to married men about their marriages, I'm in a good position to help you find out, from a man's point of view, why sex is so important to most husbands. That knowledge is not really a *secret* of happily married women—judging from the comments that women have posted on my Web site under the subject heading of "sex" (many of which are shared in this chapter), the word is out that having lots of sex to please her husband is one of the simplest things a woman can do to boost the happiness level of her marriage. Sex is, after all, the primary reason you're married in the first place.

HE ONLY MARRIED YOU FOR THE SEX

I've given a lot of thought to why people marry. It's because of sex.

That may seem like a troglodyte's view, but I don't say this to be contrary or simplistic—or even to get your attention. The history of marriage makes my point.

Centuries ago, when men and women were attracted to each other, society didn't permit them to have sex indiscriminately. It happened, of course, but the social order frowned on sex out of marriage. In fact, the only legitimate way to satisfy intense sexual desires was to marry.

Fast-forward to 2008. Now all kinds of relationships are considered permissible in American society. Sex before marriage, though still frowned on by some in our culture, holds less of a stigma now. In fact, in today's society, despite the increased risks associated with premarital sex (such as unplanned pregnancies and venereal disease), anyone can live with anyone else for any reason. Heck, lots of people choose never to marry, and they maintain a life partner for many, many years.

So why did you marry?

Some people say that they marry for companionship. But I insist that that's not a primary reason to marry. I had a houseful of male roommates when I was in college, but, as much as I grew to love those guys, I wouldn't choose them to spend my whole life with. Even if I had a roommate of the opposite sex with whom I had no sexual relationship, I can't imagine saying to her, "I'd like to be with you forever." We can have lots of companions, but we begin to think of bonding to them for life only when we have a sexual attraction to them.

True, one can look at the institution of marriage and see that this arrangement is based on more than just sex. People choose to share finances, share a home, and share family. But then why don't we "commit for life" to our same-sex best friends or close biological relatives? Because we reserve this choice for someone to whom we have a sexual attraction.

You might say that people bond for life in marriage for convenience once they get to know each other and get along. I'd agree, but again, in almost all cases that "getting to know each other" included sexual passion.

"Don't folks marry for financial reasons?" you ask. Absolutely. When we see twenty-something bombshells marrying aging multimillionaires, we can't help but wonder whether or not there might be some financial motivation. But in almost all cases I can think of, there is also some sexual attraction on the part of at least one of the parties.

We can see this in action in a little ditty about Jack and Diane. Jack meets Diane at a college social event. He's attracted to her and asks her out on a date. During the evening he realizes that she's a good match for him, and he reaches out to hold her hand, which she willingly gives him. Encouraged, he later leans forward to kiss her, and she kisses back. At each junction, he feels a rush of sexually charged energy.

After a while, despite warnings of the church and abstinence educators, Jack and Diane decide to have sex. Yada, yada, yada, it was good for both of them. Now they continue to meet, continue to date, and continue to have sex. Jack and Diane are both pretty happy with how things are going so far, and soon Diane starts to talk about possibly getting married.

When Jack doesn't respond enthusiastically, Diane says, "Tell you what. We can still be friends; we can still go to the movies together and go skiing together, but we won't be boyfriend and girlfriend—no nooky at all. I don't want to waste my time in an intimate relationship with someone who doesn't want to marry me."

Now, logically, if getting married were just about companionship or friendship, Jack might say, "Cool," and continue with everything but sex. But Jack's afraid of losing Diane, and, moreover, he doesn't want another man to have sex with her. Marriage may not have been what he was looking for when he first started dating her, but Jack knows that it's now or never. He chooses marriage because he chooses sex.

So again I say that sex is probably the primary reason you're married at all. Given that premise, it seems obvious that it should be an important—perhaps the most important—aspect of your marriage. It's certainly something that cannot be ignored when discussing the many ways to make a marriage a happy one.

HOW MEN CONNECT

If people get married for sex, what does that say about the married partners' expectation for sex once the marriage vows are made and the couple rides off with tin cans dragging from the bumper of the car?

Comedy writers of every sitcom ever made about married couples like to create punch lines that center on men who want sex and their wives who don't. In truth, men and women both want an intimate relationship, but they define intimacy in different ways. Women who tell me in therapy and on my Web site that they enjoy their sex life know that understanding the different ways males and females define sexuality goes a long way to building a happy marriage.

But if a wife does not understand this, she's apt to feel frustrated over her husband's inability to express his feelings of love without using his penis. As a woman, you, who are more intuitive, more empathic, and better able to express your love through words and nurturing gestures, probably seek and enjoy other types of intimacy and sexual connection; you like to snuggle and hug for the feeling of closeness it gives you, and you may not enjoy or certainly appreciate a quickie as an expression of deep-seated love.

I know this is likely because I spend my days listening to women talk about these kinds of feelings. I've learned that a man's way of expressing deep love and commitment can be drastically different from a woman's. And I've learned that she can easily misunderstand how important the act of intercourse is to a man's ability to feel loved and to give love.

I've also learned that women who are happy in their marriages rarely discount the importance of sex as a way for a man to attain emotional closeness to a woman.

As you read the rest of this chapter, please keep in mind that if sex is a problem area in your marriage, it's very likely that your husband is hungry to feel an intimate and meaningful connection with you. Yes, he may appear to be annoyingly goal oriented and he may totally miss your need for something more than quick orgasm-focused intercourse. But you can work with this, using your skills, your influence, and his great need to make you happy. So don't rule out improving your sex life in ways that make both of you happy; it can be an essential way of building a better relationship. In fact, you may find it's the best power tool you can use in building a strong and happy marriage.

REALISTIC EXPECTATIONS

Before we begin to talk about finding marital happiness through a mutually satisfying bond of sexuality, we need to stop right here and address an important question: In your mind, how do you picture good (that is, satisfying, bonding, fulfilling, loving) marital sex? Now ask yourself how that image compares to your real life. Does what you desire and dream of match what you get? If it does, you've already taken one big step down the path to happiness.

But if the image and reality don't match, if what you would like sex to be is not what it is, this is going to have a chilling effect on your marriage. So let's read on to find out how some women have managed to bring the fantasy of their sex life closer to reality and the reality of their sex life closer to the fantasy.

REMEMBER THIS
Sometimes It's the Man Who's Not in the Mood

The advice given in this chapter to help you increase the happiness in your marriage through intimacy and eroticism is based on two assumptions: (1) that you are in a loving marriage with a healthy male and (2) that you realize that all the secrets of happily married women work together in synergy to create that desired sense of happiness. Sex by itself can't turn an icy marriage into a hot one.

So if you have a man who's turning a cold shoulder to your attempts to heat up your marriage under the sheets and is not, stereotypically, always ready to do it in the road, there may be medical or emotional reasons that you should consider.

Sex is a complicated psychological and physiological behavior that can be affected by both physical and mental stresses. Assuming your husband is not involved in an extramarital or Internet affair, it's important to find out whether there are any medical problems that may be interfering with his sex drive. Many medications, including antidepressants and high blood pressure treatments, may impair sexual functioning. Also, if he's using alcohol or other drugs, that could explain sexual problems. Men who are depressed or who have diabetes or urological, neurological, or vascular disorders are also prone to problems with sexual performance.

SEX IN HIGH DEFINITION
AND SURROUND SOUND

Most people get their image of what sex is supposed to be like from the same place: the media. The average American is exposed to over thirty thousand television commercials a year, many of them laced with sexual innuendo. Each night when she turns on the TV, she's exposed to eight sexual situations during "family hour," and that's before she tunes into *Desperate Housewives*. If he has gone to the seven top grossing movies this year, he probably saw over fifty sexual encounters in digital color and Dolby Surround Sound. Add to that the messages on billboards, magazines, and in the newspaper, and you begin to see how our perceptions of sexual norms are shaped.

For example, picture the Hollywood version of great sex. The image is of the perfect erotic liaison. Two sweaty, beautiful bodies are wrapped together immersed in desire-driven, intensely passionate romance—usually outside of any emotional attachment. The sex is always steamy, always silent, always uncomplicated; it rarely involves married couples and always results in mutual orgasm.

This image—universal as it may be—sets a standard that no happy Main Street couple could ever emulate. The Hollywood couple is not real, and they do not convey real life. Yet when you compare scenes like this one to your own sex life . . . is it any wonder you're sometimes disappointed?

To get rid of that feeling, you'll need to follow the lead of women who have learned to ignore the media-driven preconceived notion of what sex ought to be. When it comes to great sex, you write your own script.

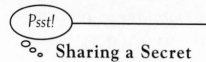

Sharing a Secret

"Frequency Is Not the Measurement of Love"

I don't have the same sex drive I did when I was younger, but neither does my husband. We've learned to accept that and recognize that frequency is not the measurement of love—but we still make sure we "do it" at least once a week.

—Kimberly, age 43, married 18 years

HOW GREAT CAN GREAT SEX BE?

Here's a questionnaire that will help you identify your own beliefs about sex and sexuality. Take a moment and answer each of the following questions. Your answers will help you see how close fantasy and reality match in your marriage:

1. Each sexual experience should involve mutual desire and arousal. __ **Yes** __ **No**

2. It is crucial for the woman to be orgasmic each time sex happens. __ **Yes** __ **No**

3. Sexually satisfied people have simultaneous orgasms at least half the time. __ **Yes** __ **No**

4. The more intimate a couple is, the more erotic the sex. __ **Yes** __ **No**

5. The man has to be receptive every time his partner initiates sex. __ Yes   __ No

6. In order to experience a positive sexual encounter, both people should be turned on before sexual touching begins. __ Yes   __ No

7. Each intimate experience that involves touch should proceed to orgasm for both partners; if not, one (or both) will feel cheated.   __ Yes   __ No

8. Fantasizing about another person usually means you want to have an affair.   __ Yes   __ No

9. Afterplay is necessary only if he or she has not reached orgasm.   __ Yes   __ No

10. Feelings of disappointment or anger must be resolved before being sexual.   __ Yes   __ No

11. If up to 15 percent of sexual experiences are dissatisfying or don't go right, this signals a major sexual problem. __ Yes   __ No

12. If one person wants to use erotic videos or sexual toys, this is a sign of lack of attraction.   __ Yes   __ No

13. As long as you love each other and keep the lines of communication open, sex will be fine.   __ Yes   __ No

14. It's better if one spouse (usually the man) is the sexual initiator.   __ Yes   __ No

15. If you aren't having sex at least three times a week, you probably have some kind of sexual dysfunction. __ Yes   __ No

The test you just took is a sexual myth test—the short version. Based on the most advanced research available, and complemented by my clinical practice, the correct answer to each of these questions is no. Believing in any of these misleading myths can interfere with your ability to get all that you want out of your sex life.

Here are the real-life facts about couple sex:[1]

- Fewer than 50 percent of couples will describe any particular sexual interaction as being mutually satisfying.

- In one quarter of all sexual liaisons, only one partner experiences sex as a positive, and the other as "just okay" or neutral. Usually, it is the male who feels more satisfied; clearly these sexual encounters are not "scene stealers."

Sharing a Secret

"I Have the Body That My Husband Loves"

I worried that the way my body changed after childbirth would turn him off, and that worry was affecting my enjoyment of our lovemaking. When I finally confessed my concern, he held me close and reassured me, telling me how beautiful I was. I think I fell in love all over again at that moment. I was finally able to relax and give him the love I wanted to. I may not have the body of a movie star, but I have the body that my husband loves and that's all that matters to me.

—Samantha, 27, married 2 years

REMEMBER THIS
Sex and Intercourse
Are Not Synonymous

When I titled this chapter "Have Lots of Sex" I didn't intend the word *sex* to be synonymous with *intercourse*. It can be if you want it to be, but many couples who struggle to create gratifying intimate connections learn that the penis and vagina are only two of many body parts involved in sex. Using all your body and your entire mind, you can remain open to many forms of sensual and sexual encounters that make having lots of sex a joy rather than an assignment.

- Fifteen percent of all sexual interactions are felt to be "passable" by couples. No complaints, mind you, but nothing that they are going to wake up in the morning with an ear-to-ear grin about.

- Five to fifteen percent of sexual experiences of normal, happy, and healthy partners are unsatisfactory or frankly ungratifying.

Keep these statistics in mind as you're tempted to keep up with the Indiana Joneses. When it comes to sex, you cannot realistically compare your activities to others—especially those in the movies. The truth is, there is not one right way to enjoy a good sexual relationship. If two people are content with having sexual intercourse once a month, then that is just as healthy as a couple who systematically achieve mutual orgasm during nightly trysts. *There is no right or wrong except for what is right or wrong for you and your partner.* To get there, ignore your TV, disregard movie romance, and close the pages of the *National Enquirer.* Truth, you will come to realize, can be so much more satisfying than fiction.

A STORY OF BIG MACS AND STEW

Although sex is not all it's cracked up to be in the movies, it is big. Studies show that in happy marriages, sex accounts for about 20 percent of the contentment that reigns within the home. When the marriage is bad, though, sex accounts for 50 to 75 percent of the cause of domestic strife.[2] This sure is strong motivation to build a happy and healthy marriage by improving the sexual relationship with your husband. Yet some women resist the idea.

As I write this, I'm reminded of a woman (a urologist no less) who, in the very first session between her, her husband, and me, stated emphatically, "And don't start telling me to have more sex; I've been to too many therapists who tried to force *that* one down my throat!"

It's clear that women do have sexual desires, but clinical experience and research show that most women look for more than a release of physical sexual tension when they are with a man (unlike many men who feel they must "do it" or explode); they are looking also for emotional fulfillment that accompanies moments of intimacy. Women don't look just for sex; they are looking for sexual satisfaction. This satisfaction is not cooked up from the single ingredient of intercourse. No, women are connoisseurs of a stew of sexuality: a dash of romance, a tease of flirtation, a drop of perfume, an act of kindness all mixed together, simmered and stirred over time until appetites are brought to a perfect pitch and the dish is ready to be consumed. So very different from the guy who throws a Big Mac on the table and says, "Let's eat."

So is there any way for the slow-cook chef and the fast-food junkie to have a satisfying meal—not just once, but over a lifetime? Yes, absolutely. But to make that happen they will each need to learn how to appreciate each other's point of view and how to mix and blend their needs so that they both are full and satisfied at the end of each meal.

Okay, enough with the food metaphor. What I'm trying to say here is that if you can find deeper sexual satisfaction and your hubby can have more intercourse with you, you will be one happy couple. How to do that is the question.

Despite all my expertise and research, I can't tell you the one right way to gain this sexual satisfaction; it's unique to you and your relationship. But I have found that women and men fulfill their desires—at whatever level that may be—when they have a good understanding of two aspects of human sexuality that can make or break the unique bond between married couples: eroticism and intimacy.

Eroticism

If, when you hear the word *eroticism*, you think of male strippers at Chippendales, don't blush! Let's face it, humans, like all animals, crave stimulation. From the first time you fantasized about sex, you felt sensual urges in your body. These feelings of physical arousal did not necessarily involve an emotional connection with another person; they might have happened while sitting alone in your bedroom.

Once you understood these sensations, you probably instinctively sought sexual release. Your sexual urges involved a deeply ingrained instinct to seek physical gratification, from saucy novels and groping in the back seat of the car with your high school date to masturbation and erotic fantasies. That's eroticism, and it's a very healthy part of your sexual self.

For adults, the sexual dynamics of eroticism usually involve nudity, with manual or oral rubbing, or, in some cases, vibrator stimulation to high arousal or orgasm for one or both partners. Other examples of eroticism include verbalizing or playing out sexual fantasies, touching yourself and having your husband watch before you invite him to join in with you.

No problem, right? Wrong. Here's the truth: Although many women have told me that accepting eroticism into their sex lives has kept their marriages happy, many other women have told me that although they know their husbands are turned on by it, they're just not comfortable with it and can't give in on this point.

Sharing a Secret

"We Enjoy a Wide Range of Things"

We've been married 20 years and for the first 10 or so, there wasn't a whole lot of experimenting going on. Gradually, though, erotic lovemaking was introduced (not sure by whom). Probably our first experimentation was reading erotic stories to each other. We have since moved into toys, shaving, etc. (I'm not getting any more specific!) And now we enjoy a wide range of things we do that we both enjoy. Instead of getting dull as the years go on, sex is getting better.
        —Lindsey, 50, married 20 years

REMEMBER THIS
There's a Reason You're in the Mood

There's much hullabaloo lately about pheromones, microscopic chemicals that cause changes in behavior through the sense of smell. We know that these chemicals will attract insects to each other over miles of terrain. It's believed that pheromones are also responsible for the ways in which women's periods synchronize when they share a dorm room. Marketers try to sell pheromones to people in hopes of stimulating sexual desire, but as one of my male clients, who has been using pheromone-laced cologne for the last two years, points out, "Women are a lot more complicated than moths." Complicated, yes, but there is fascinating research which shows that when a woman is fertile, she finds the smell of a man's sweat-soaked T-shirt attractive. The other twenty-six days of her cycle, she is repulsed by it.[3] The debate still rages about the degree to which humans are subject to the influence of unconscious passions, but such biological imperatives should at least be considered while we're on the subject of sex drive. There are sound physiological reasons why you may feel in the mood one day and not the next. When it happens—enjoy!

Why the hard line on something that could add fun and passion to a marriage? Sex educator Laura M. Brotherson says it could be because of a phenomenon she calls "The Good Girl Syndrome."[4] According to Brotherson, girls are taught that being sexual is immoral or reflective of bad character. I think she may have a point. I didn't grow up a woman, but I recall the guys' attitudes toward girls who liked sex; they wanted to hook up with these girls, to be sure, but being "loose" wasn't considered a positive character trait. That attitude pervaded the girls' culture, too, as girls passed on news about others' reputations for being "slutty." Happened in my day, and it still happens today. The message about females was clear from an early age: If you're interested in sex, you're bad. After a while, some girls accept these beliefs and begin to feel shame about their sexual drives.

It's vitally important to recognize that your marriage bed can be a safe and exciting place to learn all about your passions and desires. Being inhibited by outdated social mores that don't apply to you just stands in the way of your happiness. That need for erotic arousal is still there if you give yourself permission to let it out.

Intimacy

The second element in the recipe for getting your needs met is *intimacy*. We are animals, yes, but we're human animals, and each of us needs to meet more than our biological requirements alone. Eroticism is the physical manifestation of sexual needs. Intimacy is the spiritual component that involves a sense of emotional connectedness. When a man and a woman take the time to learn about each other's inner world and share a sense of unity through that experience, they've got the makings of intimacy.

Psst!
°° Sharing a Secret

"I'll Feel a Rush of Love"

Some days I worry that I'm not sexually attracted to my husband anymore, but then without warning, he'll put his arms around me and I'll feel a rush of love. I've learned not to panic or make quick decisions when I momentarily fall out of love. Now I trust that the feeling will return—and that often happens when we're having sex.

—Kathy, age 34, married 9 years

This isn't to say that you don't or won't recall the first time you and your husband "did it" like wild animals. But you probably also remember the long walks on the beach, the heartfelt conversations deep into the night, and the times you spent lying in each others arms, talking about your lives, the kids, the future . . . or just watching a video. *That's* the stuff of intimacy. *That's* what women tell me they crave in their relationships. Without this sense of intimacy, many women cannot move on to fulfilling intercourse with their husbands. Ah, and there is the great divide.

ENJOYING THE DIFFERENCES

Couples who wear that telling grin of the sexually happy have found a way to integrate eroticism and intimacy into their relationships that feels right for both partners. This is not always so easy to do.

Going back to the food metaphor: Most men prefer the Big Mac, which represents the immediate (but rather crude) satisfaction of sexual desire, and most women prefer the multi-ingredient stew of intimacy that needs time for simmering before it is consumed.

On the surface, the answer to this dilemma looks easy: Men, show more intimacy; women, be more erotic. But it's not always easy to do this. Once again, human biology is the instigator.

Let's use Emma and her husband, Lou, as an example. They had spent the afternoon at the funeral of Emma's boss's mother. They arrived home around noon, before the kids came home from school, and Emma headed for the bedroom for a quick nap. As her black dress fell to the floor around her feet, she turned around to see her husband grinning at her. "He had that 'Oh baby, I want you' look," recalls Emma. "Is the man crazy? I just came home from a funeral. How on earth could he think I would be in the mood for sex?"

That's the difference between the male and female view of sex right there. Because of their higher testosterone levels, most men have a stronger sex drive than women—which, yes, they can turn on in almost any circumstance because of their single-minded ability to focus on one thing regardless of what else may be going on around them. (And don't discount the erotic possibilities of seeing a black dress dropping to the floor.)

Women, in contrast, do not have the same elevated drive for the physical act of sex, but given their need to connect emotionally, do like to kiss, snuggle, and make love—but that's not the same as sex. With their stronger left brain–right brain link and more extensive connecting fibers between brain cells, females are always taking in, combining, overlapping, and thinking about many different things. For most females, the mood, the environment, and the timing all have to combine to create the emotion and affection she desires. Then, and only then, comes the desire to enjoy the physical act of sex.

The male requirements to have intercourse are so much simpler—and obviously quite different. An oft-cited study about male and female attitudes toward sex involved students on a college campus. Men and women were recruited by the researchers and instructed to approach students of the opposite sex and say, "I've been noticing you around campus. I find you very attractive. Would you go to bed with me tonight?"

Three-quarters of the men approached said yes; none of the forty-eight women did.[5] The results remained the same in other similar studies, even when the elements of fear and safety were factored in.[6] These are not surprising findings given that when asked why they engage in sex, males say, "out of need for sexual gratification, and for stress relief";[7] females say, "to share emotions and love."[8]

Is it any wonder that both men and women feel frustrated and confused when the guy wants some sex, but his wife turns him down "because I'm still angry with you for what you said about my mother yesterday"?

I'm sure even if Emma explained to Lou that she could not get in the mood after going to a funeral, Lou's male mind would immediately counter, "But you didn't even know the dead woman!" This is one area of gender differences that is bound to cause marital upset.

Your man's desire to connect with you through sex without the dance of intimacy is yet another stumbling block to sexual compatibility. Although your level of testosterone is lower than his, your level of oxytocin is higher. This is the brain chemical

REMEMBER THIS
You Don't Have to Be in the Mood to Get Started

There's no doubt that women, more then men, require environmental stimulation to get in the mood. But many have learned through experience what sound research has proven. Even when they don't feel turned on or emotionally connected (and are tempted to reject their partners' advances), they have discovered that if they say yes anyway, they soon find themselves hot with desire and enjoying the intimacy they crave.[9] So remember: Sometimes "in the mood" comes after the necking begins.

that controls maternal nurturance and empathic bonding. It fuels your need for emotional connection *before* physical connection. It fills your being with a desire for increased emotional intimacy that then leads to sexual arousal.

Men also have a supply of oxytocin that gives them that sense of emotional connectedness, but in a rather cruel twist of evolution, the level spikes at the moment of orgasm. *After* the physical act, the higher level of hormones leads to a deeper desire to form a bond with you. He feels more intimate *after* making love, not before.

Let me repeat that, because it's a biological fact and it's really important: Men feel more intimate, loving, and connected to their wives *after making love, not before*.

To compound the differences between you and your mate, your brain structure too works against sexual compatibility.

With his single-minded focus, his ability to tune out all distractions (think of his inability to discuss *anything* while he's reading the paper or watching TV), it's very easy for him to climb over the kid's toys, push the dirty dishes aside, and ask for a quickie in the laundry room overflowing with dirty clothes.

YOU COULD TRY THIS

So what's a loving couple to do when he is driven by eroticism and she by the need for intimacy? Ah, this is a surefire secret with the power to improve your love life: Cut back on the talking, withholding, and wooing.

Hold Down the Talk

Most species of the animal kingdom don't sit over candlelight talking for hours before engaging in sex. Animals sniff each other, pump up their chests or strut around in circles, and then get down to business. Ah, the simple life that is so wonderful even for humans—if you happen to be male. But I'm aware that your female biological makeup requires more. The question is how you can convey that to your man, who does, let's never forget, want desperately to please you.

In the previous chapter, we discussed the many reasons talking to men can be frustrating and ineffective in matters of the heart. Unlike females who are so verbally gifted and have interconnected brain circuits blending feelings and words, we men are more prone to be creatures of action, not words.

For this reason, talking your way through your unmet sexual needs and desires can be an ineffective way to get what you need from your man. But it is a beginning. Let me remind you, however, that the rules of Man-ese still apply: Keep the message on point, limit the range of emotion, and leave lots of time for him to formulate his responses. Remember that most men really do want to make their wives happy, and if there's a problem that they recognize they can do something about, most guys will give it a shot.

Discussions about sexual issues should come from a place of love and from a wish for maximizing the sexual experience for both of you. When you bring up the subject, here are a few tips to get what you want out of the discussion:

1. *Be direct.* Do you want your guy to slow down the mad dash to orgasm? Would you like him to wait until you feel sexually satisfied? Tell him. He cannot read your mind (or the nonverbal messages you're sending him). If you wait until the heat of the moment, he's likely to misread your intent to help him back off while you guide his hand or body position into just the right place that will drive you crazy. Instead, get more of what you want by telling him directly.

2. *Use humor.* It's a good way to ease into just about any conversation, especially about sex. There are different kinds of humor, and, if used lovingly, it can soften the edges of a discussion. Light put-downs are usually acceptable, if your guy doesn't get too defensive. Also, putting yourself down a little can be a way to signal that you don't take all this *too* seriously.

3. *Start with a positive.* All people like to be acknowledged for their good qualities; your man is no different. Tell your guy how you love it when he breathes on your neck. Make sounds of contentment when he puts his arms around you. Let him know that you appreciate him as a sexual being. With this understood, you have

a better chance of bringing up the things you'd like to change without hurting his feelings.

4. Don't be too honest. If there are things that bother you about your husband that he can't change, nothing positive can come from talking about them. Does his appendectomy scar bother you? Does he have too much hair on his chest? Let it go. Some talks end up increasing anxiety with little probability of helping the relationship.

The Problem with Wooing and Withholding

We've been inundated by a popular culture that gives us the message that one's sex life flows from natural urges. And if the mood isn't right, there's no nooky tonight. Television and radio therapy experts insist that it's the husband's job to get a woman in the mood by showering her with attention, compliments, and gifts. He's told to start first thing in the morning and make sure that his woman feels beautiful and important all day long. Moreover, this newly romantic man must, above all, not be demanding, irritable, irresponsible, or disrespectful, for any of those lapses will result in an understandable, immediate, and irrevocable (for the night, at least) end to sexual relations.

I'm not happy about where popular culture has led marriages. You're a smart woman. You know when you're being manipulated with tokens of affection that carry a price. Let's say, for example, that you complain to your husband that you can't always turn on sexual arousal at the drop of his pants—that you need to feel romantic first. He, with his male brain, will not understand why the drop of his pants isn't enough to charge up the juices, but is willing to try it your way. So he

REMEMBER THIS
Not as Seen on *Animal Planet*

Humans are animals, yes, but they're not bound by animal instincts. If that were the case, I'd walk the aisles of a supermarket and eat everything in sight, or I'd slug any person who irritated me. We are subject to a whole host of sociological and behavioral limitations that distinguish us from most other animals. Most important, humans are distinct in that we have free choice. Making love with your husband is a decision both of you make together. All the testosterone in the world doesn't excuse one human from sexually touching another human who doesn't want to be touched.

comes home the next day carrying a bouquet of flowers, which he hands to you and then drops his pants. Feel turned on now?

Of course not. The flowers were an obvious bribe, pure and simple, and you know it. This approach to improving marital sex is an attempt to address a complex emotional issue with trite, simplistic advice. An intimate connection is not something that can be bought at the corner store and gift wrapped. Although gifts that woo are nice and always welcome, most women need more than a box of chocolates to stoke up feelings of desire.

At the same time, I also don't agree with the rather popular, but hurtful and foolish, notion that some therapists espouse that couples should withdraw from sex while they are struggling to recover the romance. This plan is generally not the male's idea. Remember that far more easily than a female, he can disengage from the world around him to focus on the rush of blood he feels in his Jockey shorts. But his wife is less likely to tune out problems in the relationship, and may feel tempted to withhold sex until her husband meets her romantic expectations.

But happily married women don't adopt this attitude. They know, from some gut-level, core understanding of human relationships, that they need to continue having sex with their husbands if they hope to rekindle those intimate feelings of their early days together; this at least keeps the spark alive while they're trying to recover the flame. In a sexless marriage, that spark has little hope of surviving, and soon the couple is sitting in cold ashes wondering what happened.

Studies prove that the longer married couples avoid sex, the more difficult it can be to start up again. If you're committed to your marriage for the long run, do not avoid sex until he "gets it" and learns what you need to feel sexually aroused.

Ultimately, enjoying the fruits of a happy marriage requires you to create a situation where you can have sex that is satisfying to both of you. This means teaching your husband what you need and committing yourself to keeping a mutually fulfilling sex life at the core of your marriage. Without that, there's no marriage.

UNDERSTAND YOUR MAN

The previous chapters have all had the underlying message that happy marriages, in large part, are built on an understanding of the differences between men and women. The quality of your sex life is no different.

If I may speak for my gender, here are a few things we would like you to know:

It's not an insult when he looks at your tired, worn-down body at the end of the day and says, "Want to meet me in the bedroom?" He may seem oblivious to your need for rest and peace, or at least some foreplay, but he's simply responding to an inner need that blocks out all other distractions and focuses his mind and body on one thing: you.

It's not insensitivity that causes a man to want sex even when things are not "romantic" between you. After a disagreement, you may want him to say "I'm sorry" before you snuggle next to him, but he may need to come inside you before he feels that connection that will let him apologize.

It's not easy for him to beg for sex. Remember that men above all else seek to avoid shame. His inborn desire to ravage you every time you swish by and unintentionally show some cleavage is not a control issue; it is a wonderful sign that he is drawn to you and that he seeks a way to get closer to you. When you turn your back, or fake that you're sleeping, he takes it personally. That may not have been your intent, but it's often the outcome.

Men don't always need intercourse; sometimes a cuddle is great also. But if a man doesn't feel that there's any possibility of intercourse this decade, then he won't be able to appreciate all the pleasures of nonsexual bonding.

Guys understand that sometimes, to avoid pregnancy or to minimize discomfort during their period, some women do not want to have intercourse at certain times. But men enjoy sexual bonding through all kinds of sex, and they secretly hope that if intercourse won't happen, they may still be able to experience orgasm in some other way. Women who understand that need are not offended when their husband gives the come-hither look at a "bad" time, but instead help him out through manual or oral stimulation. These are women who have extremely grateful and adoring husbands.

Teach Him

So let's say he raises his eyebrow and nods his head toward the bedroom. Now that you've accepted his need for eroticism and have come to appreciate that his desire for sex may be based on a wish to form a closer bond to you, what happens next? You have sex right away, right? Well, not necessarily.

Understanding his definition of sex is a good start, and there will be times when you lay down because you want to make him happy. But you can also teach him to appreciate *your* definition of sex, which probably sounds something like this: intimate experiences that may or may not lead to intercourse.

For most women, sex begins in the brain, not the vagina. It is a way to attain emotional intimacy even without physical connection. Luckily, although this is not how most men see sex, you can teach your guy through your own example that sex isn't only what happens between the sheets. Show him how, if he follows your example, he can have "sex" several times every day. And as you teach through example, you will be building up a store of intimacy that will help put you in the mood when the time is right for jumping into bed. *You* know that you can have sex without intercourse; now it's time to teach him. Here are a few secrets shared by women who know how to teach their men the way back into their heart:

- Cuddle next to your guy on the couch while watching TV or a DVD. Without saying a word, sit close

and snuggle up. Nothing more; just enjoy his closeness and make him wonder what you're up to. Enjoy
the movement of his body as he breathes, allow yourself to take in his cologne. It's best to initiate this
move when someone else (such as your kids or in-
laws) are in the room, and he can't mistake the move
as an invitation to start unbuttoning your blouse.
This might confuse him at first, but after a few
sitting-close experiences, he'll relax and enjoy this
kind of sex too.

- Kiss your guy hard on the lips when you say goodbye
  in the morning. And then leave quickly. You'll have
  him thinking "What was that!?" *That*, he'll soon
  learn, is another kind of sexual connection.

- Hold his hand. Most couples start out as hand holders
  and then drop the habit. If you haven't lately, reach
  out and take his hand as you walk along a public
  street or in the parking lot as you move toward the
  movie theater or mall. This is an easy way to show
  him how to get close without being undressed.

- Rest your head on his shoulder when you're in a
  public place like the theater or even the physician's
  waiting room. It's a simple act of intimacy that solidifies a bond of connection.

- Play footsie with him while eating dinner with the
  kids or friends. Gently touch his thigh while sitting
  next to him at the company picnic. Massage his fin-
  gers up and down while sitting in the car in stalled
  traffic.

Get the idea? I'm sure you can think of lots of ways to teach your husband that sometimes sex without intercourse is a great way to bond, connect, and enjoy each other as sexual beings.

The Next Step Higher

Once he gets it that sex doesn't always have to mean pene-tration, it's time to bump up the fun with some playful but more overt types of nonintercourse sex. This move gives you a chance to really enjoy your husband for some of what attracted you to him in the first place—that sense of fun and adventure when you're together. Although such moves are playful on the surface, they serve a very serious role in giving you a chance to enjoy each other as sexual beings without having intercourse as an end point.

How do some women bump up the fun? They

- Bathe and shower as a couple.

- Call him at work and try to get him to blush (this is especially fun when his boss is standing in the room with him).

- Take out a deck of cards and challenge him to a game of strip poker.

You'd be surprised how shifting attention away from imme-diate intercourse will help him appreciate the wisdom of the saying, It's not whether you win or lose, it's how you play the game!

"But," said Maryanne when we first talked about creating her own sense of intimacy, "these are the things I want my husband to do for me. It's hardly romantic when I'm the one who has to initiate nonintercourse flirtations."

Maryanne had been married twelve years when she first stepped into my office looking for a way to rekindle the passion she missed in her marriage. I understand why my suggestion that *she* be the one to boost the level of intimacy in her marriage was a bit disappointing. She already knew how to be romantic—*he* was the one with the problem. This may be the case in your marriage too; if it is, you'll have to trust me here and accept the same advice I gave to Maryanne: Your man needs to learn these things by watching you before he can do them himself. You have the ability to make him a better lover who meets your romantic needs, if you patiently teach him how.

"But," continued Maryanne, "isn't a lot of this just titillating and teasing?"

Yes, it is. Done right and continuously, nonintercourse sex is bound to lead to intercourse. But that's the idea. It will be the kind of intercourse that satisfies the needs of both the man and the woman. Nonintercourse sex builds up sexual tension in a man that makes him crazy to have his woman in his arms; and for the woman, nonintercourse sex gives her the mental and emotional bond she often needs to be physically turned on and to enjoy the whole experience.

Jenny, one of the contributors to my Web site, knows exactly how this works. Married to Will for five years, she writes,

> Between work and raising three children, there are times when even the most erotic of intentions die out by the time we have an opportunity to actually do something more than a quick grope when the kids aren't looking. We sometimes have gone two weeks without having intercourse because by the

time we get a chance to be alone, one or both of us
is just too tired.

But Jenny has developed a broad idea about how to define
"good sex." She has learned how to enjoy the give-and-take
of a dynamic sex life, recognizing that she and Will can feel
good about their sexual connection when they are not in bed
together. Jenny points out,

There are times when we have sex two or three
times a day by doing little things during the day to

Psst!

Sharing a Secret

"We Have a Lot of Sexy Affection"

*Passion is alive and well in our marriage; in fact,
much better than in our earlier years together.
We have a lot of sexy affection throughout the day,
which really makes us feel connected and loving. If
sex has to wait a few days, we still make each other
feel desired, primarily through affection or by dressing
up. If I put on some really high heels and a short skirt
and walk around the house in them, that makes him
quite happy. I keep a bottle of Obsession perfume by
my bed. I wear it to let him know I am in the mood.
Now he sprays some on when he is in the mood, or
I spray some on him!!*

—Alice, 44, married 13 years

make each other feel sexy and desired: from em-
braces and loving words while I make dinner, to a
surprise oral sex while he is on the phone in the
den. We do these little things whenever we get the
chance. We know from the beginning that they
won't end up in full scale intercourse because there
simply won't be time, but all of those little things
build up and make us even more excited when we
finally do have the opportunity. We don't wait for
the right time for sex to show that we are turned on
by each other.

Not only have Jenny and Will found a wonderful blend of
eroticism and intimacy, they have recognized that they can do
lots of sexy things besides having his penis enter her vagina.
Hey—I'm all for intercourse. But when both partners recognize that they can feel deeply connected through a whole variety of intimate experiences, each walks away feeling more
satisfied.

The Do Less Lesson

Now you know that the intent of this chapter was not to require you to spend more time on your back to improve your marriage. With a better understanding of your man's sexual needs and your own needs, you can now start experiencing more passion and romance by doing less of what drains energy and desire out of a marriage: things like avoiding his wink and nod, dodging his hints, complaining that he sees you as an inanimate machine, accusing him of objectifying your body and not caring who you really are, or dreaming that some other lover will meet your expectations. Today, get more attention from your man by being more playful and teaching him your own definition of sex—it's 24/7 if he wants it, and it's easy and fun for you.

6

Take Charge of Your Own Happiness

A braham Lincoln once said, "People are about as happy as they make up their minds to be."

To this rather simplistic view of human emotion, I can hear women all over America saying, "That's easy for a man to say." But happily married women instinctively know that Honest Abe's words are true, and apply it to their lives every day. Despite the difficulties you face juggling the often inequitable workload of being a wife and perhaps mother or career professional (or both), you can *choose* to be happy and, by doing so, infect your husband with happiness too.

WHAT EXACTLY IS HAPPINESS?

In America, we see happiness as an inalienable right, on the same ground as life and liberty, guaranteed by the Declaration of Independence. But a more careful reading of that brilliant and subtle document says we have the right to *pursue* happiness—ah, not quite the same thing as the right to *be* happy. So let's put more focus on how to pursue that thing called happiness.

Let's first define what it is we're in pursuit of. I think we can agree that happiness is a positive emotional state that exists in varying degrees: contentment at its lowest end and euphoria at its highest.

Yeah, this is good for a textbook definition, but still it's too vague to help us go out and get a piece of it. After all, happiness is abstract, not something we can hold in our hands saying, "This. This is happiness" (except of course if that something is 3-karat diamond ring—that could be an exception).

Complicating our attempt to define happiness is the fact that this positive emotional state is produced by different things in different people. One person, for example, may find happiness at the ballet, while another finds it at a baseball game. One may find happiness in a man who is protective and attentive; another may find happiness only in a man who gives her independence and space.

For this reason, neither I nor all the happily married women in the world can tell you, "If you have this one thing, you'll have a happy marriage." But in this chapter I will share with you secrets of women who have learned to take charge of their own happiness and have achieved this wonderful state of marital bliss. You too can

1. Fully understand what marital happiness is not so that you can stop wasting time and effort on unrealistic expectations.
2. Define what marital happiness is to you and your husband.
3. Make a conscious plan to attain that happiness today.

REMEMBER THIS
Your Chances of Being Happy
Are Higher If You're Married

Only 34 percent of adults in this country say they're very happy, according to the latest Pew Research Center survey. Half say they are pretty happy, and 15 percent consider themselves not too happy. But the numbers improve for married people! Among married people, 43 percent say they are very happy, beating out the 24 percent of unmarrieds who say the same. These numbers hold up for men as well as for women, and for the old as well as the young.[1]

WHAT MARITAL HAPPINESS IS NOT

There are many myths about happy marriages. Unfortunately, believing them makes it impossible to feel happy in your marriage. Here are the five most destructive myths that I hear from women in my practice and from the many women who have responded to my surveys and online questionnaire. As you read through the next sections, ask yourself whether you've bought in to any of these myths. You may be surprised to find that in reality, marital happiness is far different from the magical image you may hold in your mind:

Marriage Myth 1: Marriage automatically makes you happy.

Marriage Myth 2: Good marriages are always passionate and heart-throbbing.

Marriage Myth 3: In happy marriages, child care and house-work are evenly distributed.

Marriage Myth 4: Both partners are responsible for the level of marital happiness.

Marriage Myth 5: If your marriage makes you unhappy, the best solution is to get out.

Marriage Myth 1: Marriage Automatically Makes You Happy

If immediate personal happiness is your priority, you may have to ditch your husband to get it. Wait! Before you send your husband packing, read on. Most happily married women know that marital happiness and personal happiness are not always the same thing. They know that in a mature and loving com-mitted relationship, personal happiness provides a strong foun-dation, but on a daily basis they choose marital happiness first.

"What!?" I hear you saying. But stay with me on this. If personal happiness were the same thing as marital happiness, then you could do whatever makes *you* happy, regardless of how it affects your husband, and everyone would be tickled pink. Let's say, just for example, that it makes you personally happy to go out with your single girlfriends three nights a week while your hubby stays at home with your children. Unless you have a very unusual husband who always and no matter what just loves this "playtime" with the kids, the thing that makes you happy would not make a great marriage booster. But it's important to you, right? So go ahead and do this, but agree that you'll do the same for him the next time he has an evening planned with friends. You're not thrilled about this, but it's a deal.

Before you accuse me of pushing back the progress of feminism, let me make clear that I do believe that after exchanging vows, your husband too is bound by the same happiness requirement: Marital happiness comes first. If his personal happiness could come first, he might say, "I'd feel much happier if I didn't have to go to my wife's family gatherings, so I'm going to work at the office instead." If you're like most wives, you'll recognize that that plan may be good for him, but obviously not so good for the marriage.

See what I mean? Saying "I do" changes the happiness dynamic. Husbands and wives have to consider how their actions and desires affect each other. They have to balance the pursuit of personal happiness with their desire for marital happiness. It is an essential truth that sacrificing one's own needs for someone else's is a necessary and worthwhile part of human relationships. When that truth is denied in a marriage, the results can be especially destructive; abandoned spouses and children get left behind in the dust of misguided soul-searching for personal fulfillment focused on ego-driven needs.

Both partners need to put the happiness of the marriage before their own happiness—but your husband may need you to lead the way. Males can be rather self-absorbed (or as some women say, selfish and self-centered) due to their brain structure, hormones, and, perhaps, their upbringing, that push them to protect and control, rather than nurture and relate. But they're quick learners, and, following your lead, your man will soon learn how to balance personal and marital needs.

While writing this chapter, my coauthor, Theresa, was struggling to keep this balance in her own marriage and found that being mindful of Marriage Myth 1 helped her improve her daily dose of marital happiness. It was a hot Saturday afternoon in early summer. She had spent all morning on the weekend chores: vacuuming, dusting, laundry, ironing, and errands. After finishing her work, she took a shower, freshened up, grabbed a large glass of iced tea and a brand-new novel she was eager to read, and headed for the lounge chair on the backyard deck. As she made her way to the back door, her husband yelled from his spot in front of the TV, "Hey, let's go play some tennis."

From Theresa's point of view, here it was: the choice between achieving personal happiness by lounging with a good book after doing family chores all morning, or achieving marital happiness by spending leisure time with her husband.

"Before working on this chapter on marriage," she told me, "I know I would have nixed the tennis idea and found my way to the deck chair. But if I say that marital happiness is my priority, and believe that spending leisure time with my husband is one of the things that adds to my store of marital happiness, I couldn't decline his request and still insist that I want a happy marriage. So the iced tea went back in the fridge, and we headed out for a quick game that was really lots of fun, and made my husband happy. I then moved our dinner time up a half hour, which gave me time to read some of that book."

Marriage Myth 2: Good Marriages Are Always Passionate and Heart-Throbbing

"I love him, but I'm not in love with him." Have these words ever crossed your lips or your mind? I'm shocked by the number of women who come to my office to talk about their marriage and repeat these words verbatim. Sometimes I wonder if my secretary, Jennifer, is giving them a script to read before they come in. I don't mean to make light of this sentiment; it does strike at the heart of so much unhappiness in marriage. So let's take a look at what these wives really mean when they talk about being "in love."

When a woman tells me she loves her man, but is no longer in love with him, it usually means that there is a strong core of connection, but not that knock-your-socks-off attraction that was there on her wedding day. It means that the wife recognizes a sense of commitment, mutual obligation in sharing household responsibilities, even a sense of trust and security. It's all there, except the raging fire of passion that also used to be there when they were dating.

The desire for this passionate love is understandable—it's an intense, all-consuming, and lusciously wondrous feeling that attracts us to our mate with a beyond-words intensity. It is, indeed, why we marry—to forever be near that person who brings us a form of happiness we feel with no one else.

Hooray for that first flush of passionate love! But here's the bad news: For almost all couples, this is a temporary state.

The happily married women whom I have counseled and who have responded to my Web site queries and national surveys seem to be very aware that romantic, passionate, all-consuming love is temporary. They understand that love goes through stages, and that a shift in the intensity of love isn't necessarily a sign that the marriage has a fatal flaw.

What exactly makes one fall in love with a particular person is a complex matter, but the impressive body of work by anthropologist and love specialist Dr. Helen Fisher from Rutgers University says that the feelings we all have when we fall in love come directly from our biological makeup.[2] I first met Helen when we were on the *Today Show* together. At the time, she was describing the biological reasons behind infidelity. A few years later, Helen released the results of her studies on what makes people fall in love and how love evolves over time, which have become oft-quoted, classic research.

A Word About Brain Chemicals

To understand Dr. Fisher's theories on the early stages of falling in love, I need to add a few words about chemical messengers (neurotransmitters) in the brain. There are billions of nerve cells throughout the body, and they are responsible for communicating information to other nerve cells about what's going on in the body. But these nerves don't actually touch each other. The tip of one nerve butts up nearly, but not quite, against the end of another, and it communicates information to the waiting nerve by releasing neurotransmitters into the space between the two cells. The brain is made up of many nerve cells, and, like other nerves in the body, they also communicate with these neurotransmitters.

Let's use the example of one type of neurotransmitter, serotonin. When the brain is feeling content and free of worry, the nerve cells release copious amounts of serotonin, so they communicate the message "Everything's okay" to the next nerves down the line. When there's not enough serotonin in this space between nerves, the person will feel depressed and nervous. Antidepressant medications (such as Prozac, Zoloft, and Lexapro) are thought to reverse symptoms of depression by generating, in effect, an increase in the brain's supply of serotonin.

There are many neurochemicals in the brain, and research points to some of these agents as responsible for the stages of love. Think back to your dating days. Remember that feeling of looking across the room at the junior high school dance and feeling a longing to meet a guy? (Now that I think about what boys looked like in junior high, maybe that's not the best example. But you get the idea.) When you feel desire and long-ing, it's because the brain is being influenced by the hormone estrogen (if you're a woman) or testosterone (in women and men). Yes, his motorcycle jacket or Rolex or deep blue eyes may also play a role in the attraction, but don't underestimate the role of brain chemicals. This is called the attraction stage, and odds are that if you're married, you've been there. So let's move on to the next phase—the stuff that romance is made of.

The infatuation phase follows. During this stage of emo-tional excitement, the brain activity and chemical body changes in both males and females are remarkably alike, mask-ing many of the biological differences we've looked at in other chapters. The normal brain activity that sparks when evaluat-ing another person in a social situation is remarkably quiet in both males and females during the altered state of new love. The neural circuits that would ordinarily point out to a woman that her loved one tends to monopolize conversations or is self-centered (or even that his nose hairs are gross) lay quiet. We are biologically given time to bond with our mate in order to ensure the survival of our species—an ingenious aspect of us humans that answers the question so many people ask when they look back and wonder, "What was I thinking?"

To compound the subterfuge, during this early stage in a romantic relationship, the sexual desires of the male and female are quite similar. Under ordinary circumstances, males have ten to twenty times more testosterone and therefore a stronger sex drive than females. But remarkably, during this stage the testosterone level in females rises and the level in males drops—creating a happy middle ground.[3]

But this state of mutual lust is short lived. Critical think-ing skills and the levels of dopamine, norepinephrine, sero-tonin, and testosterone eventually return to normal, and it's at that point that marital happiness can take a hard hit. Charlie, for example, is confused now that his wife, Debbie, has made it clear that she is no longer enthralled by his play-by-play recaps of his old fraternity days—or even by the ragged frat shirt he still wears.

"She used to love those stories!" he says with obvious hurt in his voice. "And forget our sex life. There's no chance she'd want to do it on the kitchen table or in the shower like we used to. I don't know what happened." When I meet in private with Charlie, he confesses that he's sure the love is gone.

Debbie too is worried that perhaps she married the wrong guy now that the thrill of romantic love has disappeared. "I didn't see myself as sex obsessed. But I used to feel so passionate just watching him walk into the room; it was easy to have sex with him. Now I sometimes find myself hoping he'll fall asleep before I get in bed so I don't have to hear his stupid stories or feel guilty about not wanting sex. I guess I'm not attracted to him anymore. I feel awful that I can't get those feelings back; they're gone. Is it over for us?"

Losing the thrill of passionate love is a jolt that hits almost every married couple eventually. Some hold on to the emotional excitement for several years; others lose it after only a few months, but I challenge anyone married for more than seven years (coinciding with the infamous seven-year itch) to tell me that things haven't cooled off. But, despite Debbie's concerns, that definitely does not mean "it's over." Absolutely not. In healthy marriages, the love is still there, but out of evolutionary and practical necessity, it has changed—thank goodness!

The romantic love that floods the brain with dopamine and norepinephrine causes giddiness and euphoria; the drop in serotonin level causes sleeplessness, loss of appetite, and obsessive thinking. It also robs you of critical thinking skills and drives you and your lover to seek passionate sex in any out-of-the-way closet or hallway. Such behavior would be quite disruptive to the business of life and marriage if it were a permanent state. Yes, we all love that feeling—that pounding-heart rush of new love (pushing some to seek it again and again outside their marriage), but it is unsustainable. It gets in the way of holding down a job, raising children, and turning attention to important family, community, and world matters.

Psst!

°°。 Sharing a Secret

"Coals Burn Hotter"

Don't expect marriage to be all passion, romance, and rosy. After the first few years, much of that initial excitement wears off and gives way to daily routines and comforts. This does not mean the marriage is failing—I think far too many people think their marriage is failing because they don't get all hot and bothered when the partner climbs into bed naked, every time. I think with the secure feeling of a solid marriage, the partners naturally become comfortable, even lazy, with each other. I see it as a good thing, not bad! Love progresses from heated passion to something deeper and longer-lasting. The brightest flames are exciting to watch and burn themselves out quickly— but coals burn hotter, use less fuel, and last much longer!

—Beth, married 15 years

Those who are patient with this life change (and happily married women are remarkably patient) will see that these passions transform themselves into the kind of love that holds a marriage together for the long haul. In its next stage, love pushes the brain to produce vasopressin and oxytocin—chemicals associated with feelings of attachment and contentment that encourage the sense of calm, peace, and security that couples feel with a long-term partner. This is the kind of love that is lasting and, if accepted and nurtured, will accompany you and your husband through many years of a happy marriage.

And Baby Makes Three

In the "Can I catch a break?" category of marriage, at the same time that the early-love chemicals are subsiding, many newlyweds become parents—another obstacle to romance. The extraordinary time and energy required to raise children distract many couples from the need to nurture each other. In fact, two-thirds of newlyweds who became parents cite marital dissatisfaction within three years of their baby's birth.[4] But rewarding those who are patient and persistent, marital happiness and satisfaction rise again in later life as the workload and parental responsibilities decline.[5]

It's their desire for the attachment and comfort of a lifelong love that happily married women cling to during the hectic, busy, and draining early years of marriage. They accept the truer, broader definition of love that supports their pursuit of happiness.

Marriage Myth 3: In Happy Marriages, Child Care and Housework Are Evenly Distributed

Sometimes researchers do intensive, costly, long-term studies to discover the obvious. Take for example the study published in 2002 by researchers out of the University of Michigan. Looking at the years 1965 to 2002, the research team tracked the hours that males and females spent doing household chores in the United States, Japan, Russia, Sweden, Canada, Finland, and Hungary.[6] Can you guess what they found? It's my bet that any married woman in the world could have told them what the results would show. Make sure you're sitting down for this surprising result. Throughout the world, married women, on average, do more household work than married men. I knew you'd be shocked. Okay, you can get up again.

Marriage Myth 3 must be shot down, and here's why. If it is true that housework must be evenly divided for marriage partners to find happiness, then it must also be true that there are almost no happily married women in the world! I don't mean to sound flip about this, but some things get blown out

REMEMBER THIS
Happiness in Marriage
Is a Relatively New Idea

For centuries, happiness was not a factor in good marriages. Through the ages of humankind, marriage was a practical matter that ensured social and financial security and provided for offspring. It is only over the last century that newlyweds have come to expect marriage to bring them happiness as well. Historically speaking, we're all involved in a new social experiment. We're learning as we go.

of proportion in the media through special-interest groups, and suddenly you're feeling abused, misused, and unhappy over something that women in all times and places have successfully dealt with despite not being able to "fix" it.

Many women have found ways to be very happy in their marriages despite household role inequities, yet the division of household work still fuels the demise of many otherwise happy marriages. Sadly the situation is getting worse: not the inequity in housework—that gap is actually narrowing—but the perception of the unfairness of inequity is growing and so too the unhappiness that accompanies that perception.

Here are the facts about the division of labor in modern marriages:[7]

- *First the good news:* The amount of housework considered "woman's work" (such as making meals; washing dishes; providing child care; and doing cleaning, shopping, and laundry) tackled by husbands has increased since 1965—moving from twelve hours a week to sixteen hours a week.

- *More good news:* The housework hours for wives has declined sharply since 1965.

- *Not-so-good news:* Women are still stuck with a weekly twenty-seven-hour household workload—eleven hours more than their husbands.

That not-so-good news explains why despite the decrease in actual work hours, the disenchantment over this inequity has increased among young wives over the years: A growing number of women are doing more household work than their husbands *and* working full-time outside the home. In 1976, less than one-third of young mothers went back to work. Now, for the first time, a majority of new mothers remain on the job.[8]

If you're one of these working moms, you don't need me to explain how hard this can be. Trying to be a responsible employee and a committed spouse and parent is far more difficult for women than men—and again we can look to evolution and body chemistry for the reason.

Helen Fisher reminds us, "In every culture in the world where anthropologists have looked, in 168 societies, even where women are exceedingly economically powerful, women do the vast majority of the raising of the very small children. Women are interested in babies. They bear the babies. They've got the high levels of estrogen associated with the nurturing of the very young."[9] They just can't easily hand over that desire to be a good mother to anyone else. No matter how modern and helpful the dad, he's just not the woman of the house.

Unhappy Wives

Sadly, nature's pull to nurture home and hearth, and the modern family's push to have mom contribute to the family's finances have yanked women in opposing directions. Not surprisingly, something's got to give. Unfortunately, that something is often a woman's sense of happiness.

Two sociologists from the University of Virginia, Bradford Wilcox and Steven Nock, published a portrait of happy marriage. Using data from five thousand couples in the National Survey of Families and Households done in the 1990s, they found that "Wives who work full time and have more progressive attitudes are more likely to be unhappy with the division of housework. And that spells trouble for them and their marriages."[10]

That's not at all what your mother's generation expected to come out of the feminist movement. The long battle to give women the right to move their interests outside the home wasn't supposed to make you unhappy. But women who have shifted to the more modern "do it all" lifestyle have not necessarily found greater fulfillment. Surprisingly, even now, more than forty years after the publication of *The Feminine Mystique* in 1963, ample research finds that women who are happiest in their marriages are the ones who see themselves in the traditional role of nurturing caregiver—even if they work. And surprisingly, even though these women do more work around the house, they perceive their husbands as pitching in to the best of their abilities.

Working full-time and making the same or more money than one's husband increase the level of unhappiness. Among women with jobs outside the home, the happiest were those whose husbands earned at least two-thirds of the household income. The researchers who came to this conclusion suggest that there may be several reasons for this:[11]

1. Women may invest more in marriage when they earn less than their husbands.

2. High-earning women may work harder but still do the bulk of the domestic work—with resentment.

3. Unequal finances may allow for a clearer division of roles and so less day-to-day stress about whose turn it is to do the school run or get the shopping done.

If you're the CEO of a Fortune 500 company, it's unlikely that after reading this information you'll immediately inform your husband that in order to find marital happiness you each have to make a major career change. No, I'm not suggesting that you quit a high-paying job in the hopes of finding that illusive thing called happiness. But these kinds of studies give us important insight into the dynamics of marital happiness— and give us concrete reasons why the higher your level of achievement, the higher the level of your marital discontent- ment may be. But you probably suspected that. Being the breadwinner in the family as well as the cook, maid, and nanny is stressful, especially in traditional households where the burden of child care and housework still falls heavily on the female—despite the fact that the highly paid female CEO can afford to hire more help, but often does not.

Happy Husbands

Unlike married women, whose happiness quotient has gone down over the years since they won the right to "have it all," married men are just about as happy now as they were in the 1970s.[12] Compared to their fathers, they've improved in their willingness to attempt an equitable distribution of household work, but they haven't offered up their core identity. Their evolution-driven body chemistry and early childhood learn- ing has made them secure in their role as protectors and providers, even while now pitching in around the house—al- though not necessarily in ways that meet the modern wife's expectations.

Surveyed women believe that their men do a small fraction of the housework, but in fact, husbands do 70 percent of "men's work," such as trash disposal, yard work, home and auto repair, and handling finances.[13] And attempts to breed sensitive men who take on a equal share of the washing, cleaning, ironing, cooking, and child care have been moder- ately successful, making today's dads far more involved with their children and home than in any previous time. In the last twenty years, I have met very few fathers who don't know how to change a diaper—but whose own fathers didn't have a clue. Accolades aside, a common marital complaint in most homes—that the woman is still the chief cook and bottle washer—remains undeniably true.

Certainly there are husbands who carry a full 50 percent or more of the child-care and housework responsibility (I know; you're thinking, Could I have one of those?!), but the belief that the child-care and housework load must be evenly distributed is a destructive myth that encourages unrealistic expectations. Given the large group of happily married women all over the country whom I've had the honor of talking to and sharing stories with over the last twenty years, this imbalance is not an insurmountable obstacle to marital happiness. Most happily married women have found ways to deal with the inequity as a tradeoff for something they want even more—a happy marriage.

In response to my question, "What is the secret of your happy marriage?" Elaine wrote to me about how she handles the workload inequity in her marriage. She began by explaining that now in her second marriage she is learning from her past mistakes and now tries to pick her battles. Not everything, she says, is worth an argument:

> With my first marriage, it used to drive me insane that my ex expected traditional roles—my job to do laundry, cook, clean, etc. while his job was to fix cars, cut the grass, and um . . . well that's about it. We both worked, so I expected him to help with the cleaning and cooking—oh, the arguments over that! My new husband is also traditional in this way

(although he's more willing to cross the line when I ask him). But now I guess I've mellowed a bit; even though the expectation that I'll do all the housework still bothers me—I don't make such a big deal about it. Just the other day, he woke me up early on a Saturday morning asking, "What's for breakfast?" I got really angry and snapped, "I dunno . . . whatever you want to fix I guess!" And then he said, "I don't have any clean underwear." And still with my head under the pillow I said, "Hmmm, last time I looked, the washer was still in the same place as last time. Think you can find it?" We had the makings of a really good fight going that could easily have ruined the whole day.

But then I thought about what's really important to me and I got up, fixed him breakfast, and put in a load of laundry. I know the great things we have in this relationship aren't worth losing over who fixes breakfast or does the laundry. To be very honest, I don't mind doing all that stuff myself, because it does keep peace in the house, he does usually show his appreciation, and I know it makes him happy and comfortable—and therefore, me too.

Now that I'm older and more seasoned, I realize the things that used to bug me in my younger years aren't such big issues after all. Many things are worth just letting go to keep peace and harmony, even if I don't agree. I know he does the same thing for me.

An important word here: I don't share Elaine's story because I want to push women back into the kitchen barefoot and pregnant. Perhaps if I were a woman, you'd be less suspicious that I might have an agenda to get wives to serve their guys hot breakfasts and clean underwear. I quoted this real story from a happily married woman because the only agenda I have here is your happiness and helping you find it with less emotional turmoil and more positive affections.

Marriage Myth 4: Both Partners Are Responsible for the Level of Marital Happiness

"You've got to be kidding!" one of my female clients said with a sarcastic laugh when I suggested that wives of grouchy husbands can find ways to make them happy. "Let him figure out for himself how to be happy. That's not my job."

No, I'm not kidding. Let's look at the fictitious marriage of Jasmine and John to see how some women get their men to be happy. Let's say John is generally unhappy—not that he's unhappily married, but according to Jasmine, he seems too serious and blah most of the time. The mood-contagion effect can work in one of two ways, each creating a self-perpetuating cycle:

Approach 1: After years of nagging John to lighten up and of complaining about his dour moods, Jasmine unconsciously takes on her husband's mood and finds herself moping around, filled with resentment and a strong sense that her marriage is making her very unhappy. "How can anyone be happily married," she might say, "to someone who's so chronically miserable?" In turn, John will no doubt notice his wife's discontent and consider her the cause of his own unhappiness. If this situation were to come out at one of my counseling sessions, Jasmine would explain that she's unhappy because John's so unhappy. And undoubtedly

John will insist that he's unhappy because Jasmine is so unhappy. And the cycle continues.

Approach 2: When Jasmine realizes that she cannot make her husband happy by nagging or complaining, she decides to take charge of the mood that pervades her marriage and makes a conscious effort to build both personal and marital happiness for herself. As her home begins to fill with her positive energy, her own sense of fulfillment and happiness infects her husband, who will then spend less time in his introspective, serious moods—making both of them more happy.

Psst!

Sharing a Secret

"The Secret Is to Focus on Yourself"

The happiest married women are those who have learned the secret of how to change their spouse. The secret is to focus on yourself and how you can change your own thoughts, beliefs, words, and behaviors. A wife can change a relationship for the better if she keeps her focus on improving herself—like being on a continual self-improvement program. Any positive change in behavior or response to one's spouse automatically brings about a change in the dynamics of the relationship. It can help break a downward spiral to get couples back on track, or keep them moving forward toward a more connected and fulfilling relationship.

—Lynn, 38, married 16 years

Which way would you choose? The happiness level in your home begins with you. You can keep the level high by doing less worrying and complaining about your husband's moods and instead putting your energies into what is good for both you and your marriage. Your husband may not know why he's suddenly feeling happier, but you will know that by taking control of your own need for happiness, you have made your man feel happier too—and that increases the level of marital bliss for both of you.

Marriage Myth 5: If Your Marriage Makes You Unhappy, the Best Solution Is to Get Out

Agree or disagree: "Divorce is usually the best solution when a couple can't work out marriage problems." In 2006, the Centers for Disease Control reported the answers to this question after polling more than twelve thousand people. How would you guess the majority answered?

If you consider the soaring divorce rate in which half of all marriages fall apart, the results are not surprising: a full 44 percent of men and 50 percent of women agreed with the statement. That leaves far too many people ready to throw down the "D" gauntlet when times get tough, and interestingly it's women who do the throwing more often than men.

We already knew that women initiate most divorces,[14] but despite common beliefs about the major causes of divorce, male misbehavior, such as nonsupport, desertion, domestic violence, or alcoholism, is not among them. The top three reasons cited by women who initiate divorce are (1) "gradual growing apart, losing a sense of closeness," (2) "serious differences in lifestyle and/or values," and (3) "not feeling loved or appreciated by my husband."[15]

At first glance, these may seem like just causes for ending a marriage. More than likely, a good number of my readers who are in their second (or third) marriage may read these reasons and say, "Yes, that was the problem in my first marriage." If you did leave a marriage for one of these reasons, I won't hold it against you. But let's take a careful look at these causes of divorce.

When partners "grow apart" from each other, it can be very disconcerting. But growing is a part of all human development. We don't stop in our tracks the minute we take our vows. So if we must grow, what are the odds that we will grow in exactly the same direction? None—not even identical twins grow in the same direction. When people split for this reason, what they are really saying is, He (or she) is not growing in *my* direction. In order for me to be happy in the marriage, I need him to be like *this*, and instead he's like *that*!

I understand the complaint of "differences in lifestyles or values," especially when it pertains to one partner who continues to be a big partyer (read: is a drug and alcohol user) and the other who has gone straight. Certainly, when destructive behavior invades marriage, there is often no alternative than to head for the door. But the majority of people who endorse this reason for dissolving the marriage aren't referring to injurious behavior.

What kind of shift in values are they talking about? Did one suddenly shift from being a liberal Democrat to a conservative Republican? Did one suddenly start to take an interest in witchcraft? Did they flip-flop on their position on the flag desecration amendment? No. In actuality, they are referring to differences in values about such things as whether and where they should spend money and how to raise the children.

Needless to say, no two folks will agree on all these matters. Being of different minds is an opportunity to learn how to compromise and see another point of view. But when men and women leave marriages because they feel that their perspective isn't appreciated, it means that they view this as an affront to their peace of mind, their inalienable right to be right. They walk away from marriage because they are no longer feeling happy about the relationship. Conveniently, "I'm not happy" falls under the umbrella of what we euphemistically call "no-fault divorce."

Assuming infidelity, violence, or addiction are not the problem, Marriage Myth 5, above all others, is the greatest cause of unhappiness in marriages. Having the escape valve always at the ready—if he doesn't shape up, I'm out of here—is no way to make a marriage work. Happily married women and men know that marriage really is "forsaking all others till death do us part," and therefore are not willing to give up when the initial euphoria fades away and daily life struggles seem to sap the joy out of eternal commitment.

These feelings of unhappiness are true and honest expressions of personal distress—but I've got to tell you that they're no reason to break the marriage vows. Even though our no-fault system says we can split up for no apparent reason, I have to say that doing so is downright selfish. Remember, much like the Declaration of Independence, marriage doesn't guarantee happiness, but rather offers each of us the right to pursue it and a forum in which to do so. When times get tough, when romantic love dims and when the stresses of daily life seem overwhelming, that's not the time to cut and run; that's when the couple has to make the effort to keep the marriage intact. In fact, it is often an opportunity to grow and work with your partner to create an even stronger—and happier—marriage.

Psst!

✺ Sharing a Secret

"Soon Things Will Be a Ten Again"

A happy marriage is when you fall back in love after you think you have fallen out of love. It's when you choose to stay rather than go after an argument. Sometimes I think I have a happy marriage and other times I think it could be better. But one thing I can say when I am unsure if I am truly happy is that I still love him and care about him. On a scale from one to ten, I have ten when things are going great. When things aren't going so great, it is probably around three to five. During those times, I remind myself to be a little bit more attentive, patient, and loving, and soon things will be a ten again. I guess I classify a happy marriage as something that is not always going to seem happy, but really is if you stick around through the hard times.

—Jayne, 43, married 13 years

During these periods of unhappiness, couples determined to honor their vows often find fulfillment in their marriage by focusing on the indirect benefits of being married. They may like the financial advantage, the social comfort, the family security, or even the ready availability of STD-free sex for procreation or recreation. They recognize that, statistically speaking, their children will be more confident in their own lives, do better at school, and have a better chance of staying married themselves. These very positive aspects of marriage are often enough to keep the couple together long enough for the spark to return—especially if the wife takes the lead.

Because women are the ones who register the most complaints in marriages,[16] those who choose instead to focus on the positive, often find that their husbands appreciate the effort and begin to meet more of their needs over time. This is very likely why researchers have found that wives who believe in marriage "as long as you both shall live"—rather than marriage "as long as you both shall love"—are happier.[17]

WHAT IS HAPPINESS FOR YOU?

Knowing what happiness is *not* is a good start in securing your place as a happily married woman. I hope it helps, but I do realize that it's bad form to describe something by what it's not. If I told you that a hammer is not a screwdriver, it still wouldn't really tell you what you need to know about a hammer. So the question remains: What *is* happiness?

You'd think that as a psychiatrist with over twenty years of clinical experience I'd have the definition by now—but I don't. My years of talking to women (and being married to one) have taught me that there is no one thing that makes women happy. And I'll bet your husband has no real grasp of what makes you happy either, but if you identify exactly what it is and tell him directly, he'll soon catch on.

In the next chapter, we'll look closer at the physical, emotional, and spiritual support you need as a woman to sustain marital happiness.

The Do Less Lesson

Happiness is elusive when you try to have it all, all at once. Because you can't make all people happy all the time, decide what you can do to make you and your husband feel a moment of joy today—put that on top of your to-do list. Make marital happiness your top priority and let go of the other stuff that clogs up your day.

7

Heal Thyself

M uch of this book has focused on getting more out of your marriage by adjusting your style of living to accommodate and encourage that very peculiar and wonderful man called "husband." You know he wants to please you, and you know how to help him be a better man.

But at the same time, you must never forget that you have many strengths, sensitivities, and sensibilities that are yours alone through and through and have nothing to do with being a wife. So, in this last chapter, it's time to follow the lead of the women who know that finding a sense of balance between one's personal life and marital life, is the real secret of fulfilling happiness.

TAKE OFF YOUR CAPE

Women today can and do have it all—including exhausting schedules that often trample all over personal needs and desires. Yet some remarkable women find ways to keep their cool in the midst of seemingly unending demands. Thirty-four-year-old Toni, for example, finds pleasure in her busy life, but draws the line at playing Superwoman.

"When I graduated college," Toni remembers, "my girl-friends and I dreamed of having perfect careers, perfect children, perfect husbands, and being perfect human beings. For years I tried to achieve those dreams." Toni goes on to describe how she married, moved to an affluent suburb, got a great job, and had two wonderful children. Then she began the juggling act in this quest to have it all: driving the children to play-groups and ballet; picking up and dropping off for soccer and t-ball; talking to teachers, coaches, and religious school instructors. Toni also got involved in the regional domestic violence awareness program, continuing education classes for her career, and decorating the new addition to her home. And of course there were always the usual domestic chores of laundry, shopping, meal preparation, dishwashing, and dog walking. Oh yeah, and then there was her husband.

"It didn't take me long to realize that I couldn't possibly attain the highest achievement in everything if I wanted to keep my sanity and my marriage. I forced myself to step back, identify the things that were my can't-live-without priorities, and let go of the rest. Now, we are all much happier."

Toni says she's watched some of her good friends become overwhelmed as they struggle against the social pressure to do it all. "I've watched them burn out and turn to therapists, anti-depressants, and even divorce to find happiness—but they don't find what they're looking for."

No doubt about it, things have changed for American women in the last half century. In many ways, these changes have been good, as women now have doors open to them that their grandmothers never had. But those opportunities come with a price. Since the feminist revolution, women have been told that they can have all they want. Unfortunately, the message has been distorted to say that they should *want* to have it all.

Toni is a good example of a woman who knew that in order to find peace and happiness in her life and in her marriage, she needed first to step back and take care of herself. Now it's time for you too to put aside the inspiring but dangerous notion that you have to have it all to be accomplished, successful, and happy. Paradoxically, the better you take care of yourself, the more you will have to give back to others.

That's why happy wives are first of all happy human beings. You cannot feel resentful, victimized, angry, lonely, or depressed as a person and then turn around and expect to be a happily married woman. It's impossible. So you have to find ways to increase your level of personal happiness in ways that support your marital happiness. When these two invaluable aspects of your life work in synergy—then you really will have it all.

ATTRIBUTES OF HAPPY WOMEN

So what does a happy woman look like? Geraldine Bedell explored this question in her study, appropriately called "What Makes Women Happy?"[1] After extensive research, analysis, and survey, she has come to the conclusion that there are typical traits that the happiest women share, including these four:

1. Being surrounded by friends
2. Being physically active
3. Being involved in life
4. Being open to spirituality

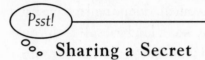

Sharing a Secret

"I Am Happy with My Life"

I think happiness plays an important role in your mar-
riage, but happiness with each other grows through the
years only when both partners feel fulfilled as human
beings. What makes me happy as an individual com-
plements my happiness as a wife. I am happy with my
life, and my marriage. I married the most awesome,
romantic man that I've ever met.

—*Tammy, second marriage of 2 years*

Using these conclusions, you can rate your own present
level of happiness and make plans to secure what you have or
to reach out and grab on to more.

Being Surrounded by Friends

When you go off on your honeymoon, you adopt the saluta-
tion "Mrs.," taking on a new identity, a new family, and often
a new home. At that point, many couples say that their marriage partner is their best friend. That's a wonderful sentiment, but it doesn't diminish the need for other friends
outside the marriage. Socializing offers opportunities for
laughing, relaxing, and sharing good feelings that are not
readily available every day from within the marriage. That
says nothing negative about the quality of the marriage. It's
just a fact: Most of us need other human beings to fill out and
balance our lives.

This is especially true for women. Even the best husband can't fill the role of confidant and friend as well as another woman can. A female friend will share your desire to chat about "nothing." Men tend to find this confusing. A female friend will listen and empathize when you're down. Men tend to look for quick solutions and have trouble being emotionally empathic. A female friend has lower expectations and more patience than most husbands and so offers an oft-needed refuge. In fact, spending time with a good friend is good for your marriage because it is apt to offer certain types of emotional help and support that your husband may not be capable of giving.

So as you seek to heal yourself when you're feeling overwhelmed, neglected, or just plain tired, looking outside your marriage to your family and friends is a positive way to help yourself. Here are a few tips to help you get the most out of your friendships:

1. *Seek friends with positive attitudes toward marriage.* I recall the time that my wife was talking to a twice-divorced friend about some of our marital problems (yes, even I have marital problems). This friend gave the advice that fit her own experience best. Can you guess what it was? Yup, she told Susan that she was a fool to put up with me and should get a divorce. I don't blame the friend; it's what she knows. But you can rest assured that if you spend a lot of time with friends who have looked toward ending marriage as a way of solving problems, you'll be more inclined to change your locks than change your approach.

2. *Enjoy the freedom of sharing with your girlfriends, but. . . .* Try to avoid sharing those conversations with your

husband. If you start a sentence by saying, "Well, I discussed our kid's problem with Elizabeth, and she thinks . . . ," your husband may feel defensive and ganged up on (unless Elizabeth is your child's pediatrician). Most men don't have frequent opportunities to talk about their home lives with friends, so they often don't receive the support on difficult issues that you might. This gets especially dicey when you offer up a friend's opinion about what's wrong with *him*!

3. *Be cautious of male friends*. Women are engaging in extramarital affairs at much higher rates than in the past, and

---

Psst!

⁰₀₀ Sharing a Secret

"Your Friends Are Invaluable"

I fell in love, got married, had a baby, but always managed to keep my girlfriends and they are such a blessing. There are things your husband cannot or will not help you through—post-partum depression, menopause, the urge to have another baby or adopt a puppy. Your friends are invaluable no matter how in love you are. I have worked hard to incorporate my husband into the lives of my girlfriends with their husbands or by telling him what is going on with them. I include him in this aspect of my life; it is not secret so when I need them, and it has happened, he knows I need them and gives me all the space I want.

—Dawn, 36, married 6 years

---

the workplace is the most common place to find a new lover.[2] You may feel that sharing intimate details of your life with your cubicle mate is legitimate because neither of you is looking for anything more than support. But it might not be long, in such situations, before you begin to feel that this attentive gentleman cares about you more than your own mate does. This is exactly the kind of comfort that can lead to a lunch together, a friendly brushing of your elbows as you pass by . . . you get the picture. You may not intend a friendship with a male to evolve into something more, but it's a real possibility for him. Studies have shown that men are much more likely to view casual connections with women as destined to lead to a sexual tryst. Any man that you spend time with should be well known by your husband; he should support your marriage and your choice to be faithful to your husband.

4. *Be wary of e-friends.* I've had many clients who have benefited from the support and nurturing found on online message boards and chat rooms. It can be a great way to find like-minded individuals. But you don't need me to tell you about the possible downside; you've seen the warnings on *Nightline* and the nightly news. Internet friendships may seem very intimate, and you may feel that the person (woman? man? computer program?) on the other end really understands you, but you should be wary of any person whose identity you can't verify, and involve your husband in any online friendships.

5. *Don't trash your husband.* Friends and family can be extremely helpful in getting you through the tough times. But even though you might feel some relief if you

tell them about all your husband's problems, you will probably also notice how they glare at him the next time you're at a dinner party. There are some things you should get support with (for instance, if you're the victim of adultery), but if you routinely put down your husband, don't be surprised if the people who love you don't support your marriage.

Being Physically Active

Yes, yes, I know you're active all day long running from one place to another and lifting groceries, laundry, and children. That's not the kind of active I'm talking about. Simply put, physical activity unrelated to work or home can increase your level of happiness.

There are lots of good reasons why exercise makes sense. Sustained, vigorous exercise in which you are able to raise your heart rate to one-and-a-half times its normal rate for more than fifteen minutes helps release those mood-elevating chemicals called endorphins. It regulates the body systems to better handle stress and has even been known to boost self-esteem in females. Studies have also shown that the effects of regular exercise can equal those of antidepressants in lifting depressed moods.[3] And, as a bonus, many forms of exercise get you out of the house and away from any negativity that may be pulling you down.

In addition to the emotional and mental benefits, being active is also a great way to stay physically fit and keep off excess weight. I know I tread on dangerous ground here, but in a book about happily married women, I cannot ignore the effect of excessive weight gain on the health of a marriage. Certainly it's easy and safe to say that taking care of yourself physically can lead to a better sense of self and a longer and more productive life on earth. But can it also help your marriage? In some marriages, the difficult, but hard-to-deny, answer is yes.

A study of 288 husbands conducted by Neil Chetik found that changes in wives' body size really did affect men: "Most married men aren't looking for their wives to stay—or become—perfect 10s forever after," he noted, "but they also don't expect their wives to stop taking care of themselves. The issue for many men is not primarily fat, but betrayal. Men are often criticized for being romantic before the wedding, then ending all romance after the wedding. Likewise, women will get criticized for caring about sex (and sexiness) before the wedding, then growing cold—and big—afterward. While weight-gain is not a make-or-break issue in most marriages, women who take care of themselves, and feel good about their bodies, are a lot more attractive to their men."[4]

REMEMBER THIS
Challenging Activities Are More Fun Than Passive Activities

University of Chicago psychologist Mihaly Csikszentmihalyi discovered that people felt happier, stronger, more creative, and more satisfied when engaged in activities involving challenge and skill. Passively watching TV conferred less happiness than driving, playing a game or musical instrument, or working.[5] Any activities or challenge in your life? For starters, pick up a crossword puzzle and see what happens!

When Geraldine Bedell asked women what made them happy, they answered "being active." It's not a stretch to assume that these women felt positive about their lives because the physical activity made them feel good about their body size, and this made their men happy too. So whether you decide to take a brisk walk every night or buy (and use) a gym membership, you will find life looking rosier when you make physical activity a part of your life routine.

Being Involved in Life

Get out of the house—and out of yourself. I know; of course you are busy "doing" things all day long, and on the rare occasion when you have a free afternoon, you just can't get yourself off the couch. Perfectly understandable. But if you've begun to make a habit of doing nothing whenever you can, you may be reducing your happiness quotient.

To stay happy, we all need to be more actively engaged in something that takes our minds off all the nagging negatives of our relationships and work problems. Dwelling on every cross word and inconsiderate action in a marriage is a plan for distress. When life seems too filled with drudgery, giving some of our time and self to activities outside our marriage, kids, and job redirects our focus to something bigger than ourselves— and builds a store of happiness that can hold us in times of a marital lull.

Bedell herself says, "Contrary to everything we're told by the self-help books, the key to happiness is not to examine your innermost self, to study your soul and think of yourself as a project to be worked on and enhanced. We are most likely to be fulfilled, and so happy, by getting involved in something bigger than ourselves. . . . Happiness, it seems, is losing yourself in something, or someone, else."[6]

It's possible that this something is a larger cause—perhaps building a school playground, expanding the recycling program in town, promoting voter registration, or simply volunteering in the local library. Or it can be a personal passion that you'd given up in your desire to focus your time on your family. Perhaps it was the joy of playing a musical instrument? Or cross-country skiing? Or needlepoint? Or simply reading a good book? For your own sake and the sake of your family, revive that interest so that you can feel involved in an activity that is not on your list of chores and responsibilities.

That's exactly how Melinda heals herself whenever her world gets too demanding.

"I'm a giver," says Melinda, a mother of three adult children, who now helps care for her nine-month-old granddaughter.

> I'm so used to helping other people that I never really thought to do something just for myself. But when I was cleaning out the back corner of our basement last year, I found my old paint easel. I was suddenly filled with this longing to paint again. Gee, it had been twenty years since I had gone off on my own to capture a landscape on canvas. Now, I've reclaimed that part of me and I feel like an entirely new person. I have an outlet when I feel angry or frustrated. Just knowing that I'll be able to grab my paints for an hour on the weekend gives me something to look forward to all week long.

And how does Melinda's husband feel about this? He loves it. Like most husbands, he's preprogrammed to seek his wife's happiness. So when she's in full bloom, he relaxes and actually is inclined to take credit for her happiness, as in "See what a good husband I am; I have such a contented wife!" Melinda isn't offended by the sentiment; she accepts that it is a way for everyone to reap the benefit of her decision to look outside her home for an occasional escape.

Being Open to Spirituality

You know that there's more to this life than finding a good parking spot, that there are reasons for living beyond getting the proposal done for your client by week's end, and that you have some basis to be on this earth besides remembering to place a check in your kid's backpack for her school field trip. But too often, women tell me that they are so busy juggling all the day-to-day demands of life that they just don't seem to be able to see the big picture.

Yet one of the most powerful ways for women to regain their strength and find balance in their lives is through reconnecting with their spiritual side. One of my clients, Yvette, talks about the stresses of her husband's unemployment as she struggles with an ill mother who lives seventeen hundred miles to the south in Puerto Rico. When I asked how she copes, she said she goes to church every Sunday and meets with a prayer group weekly.

No, it's not the same as sitting by her mother's sickbed, and it doesn't bring in extra income, but it gives Yvette a chance to take a step back and see the big picture. "I'm reminded each time I pray of my many blessings; it brings me a sense of calm."

For some, spirituality finds its home in the walls of a religious institution; for others, it can be found through personal meditation. Dr. Herb Benson, who is credited with introduc-

Psst!

Sharing a Secret

"I Just Plain Talked Out Loud to God"

*My husband had a 2-year affair. When I knew in my
heart he was going astray, I turned everything over to
God. I asked God to stay with both of us and to show
me a way in which I could stand back and let my
husband do what he thought he wanted to do. The
hurt from the affair was/is unbelievable. My intuition
kept telling me we still loved one another and so I
stayed in the marriage. I waited and followed God
and my heart. We still have a distance to go, but I
believe we will make it. I see him working on this
problem daily. I kept the home and four children and
worked fulltime as a nurse; he is in sales, and had
way too much time away from home and too much
free time when he was gone. Recently, he has changed
territories and this has been a key move. I am happy
to be married, and happier that I asked God for help.
Actually, I just plain talked out loud with God daily,
and when people would ask to whom I was talking,
I just smiled and said, "my Best Friend."*

—Aimee Lee, 40, married 18 years

ing a westernized version of Transcendental Meditation with his book *The Relaxation Response*, uses scientific studies to prove how important a spiritual life can be. An independent experiment found that when workers in a company were given an eight-week course in meditation, their scores went up an average of 20 points on a 0–100 scale of happiness.[7]

There surely is a connection here. Writing about Benson's work, authors Kiesling and Harris note: "People high in spirituality (which Benson defines as the feeling that 'there is more than just you' and is not necessarily religious) score high in psychological health. They also have fewer stress-related symptoms and show the greatest rise on a life-purpose index as well as the sharpest drop in pain."[8]

So whether you find spirituality in an organized religion, or in a dedication to yoga or meditation, or in a strong attachment to nature, the belief in some higher power beyond the self that benevolently guides your life is key in the pursuit of happiness.

HOW HAPPY ARE YOU?

If you aren't as happy as you would like to be in your marriage, a general sense of discontent may be the reason. Take a minute to evaluate the role of the four happiness producers in your life with this quick quiz. Circle the answer that best describes your situation:

Happiness Calculator

1. Friendship

At this time, I do things with my friends:

a. never

b. twice a year

c. once a month

d. weekly

e. almost every day

2. Physical activity

At this time, I am physically active:

a. never

b. once a season

c. once a month

d. weekly

e. almost every day

3. Involvement in life

At this time, I am involved in activities outside my home and job:

a. never

b. once a year

c. twice a year

d. once a month

e. at least weekly

4. Spiritual life

At this time, I meditate or seek refuge in a higher power:

a. never

b. once a year

c. once a month

d. weekly

e. almost every day

Find Your Happiness Quotient

Score your responses using this point system:

0 points for every "a"

1 point for every "b"

2 points for every "c"

3 points for every "d"

4 points for every "e"

High happiness quotient: 13 to 16 points

In your personal life, you have all the pieces in place that can then be brought back into your marriage to help you truly be a happily married woman.

Medium happiness quotient: 9 to 12 points

Your well of potential happiness has room for more! You should look at each happiness target that is not strong in your life right now and make a plan to increase your involvement.

Low happiness quotient: 0 to 8 points

It's time for you to choose happiness over some of your other "must-dos" each day. Your mental health and the future of your marriage require this shift in focus.

The Do Less Lesson

Yes, you can have it all—but think twice before you decide that you want it all. In the rush to do, get, achieve, please, and succeed, something important can be lost—you. And if that happens, no one in your family will be truly happy. And as the good witch explains to Dorothy—the happiness you're after has been there all along; you just need to learn where to look for it.

I have no doubts that you can find happiness in your marriage without sacrificing who you are in the process. As you use your inborn abilities to forge a solid and loving bond with your husband, he'll develop a growing respect for your womanly gifts and will play a more active part in forming a spectacular partnership with you. He wants to please you. He wants to be your partner, help you meet your own life goals, and become your best fan. And as a team, how can you lose?!! This is happiness.

Epilogue

When Mamma's Happy,
Everybody's Happy

There is no happiness like that of being loved
by your fellow-creatures, and feeling that your
presence is an addition to their comfort
—*Charlotte Bronte*, Jane Eyre

The decision to join with one man for the rest of your life is daunting. But it's nothing compared to the challenge of *keeping* a relationship with that man—a relationship that will provide both of you with a life of excitement, passion, tenderness, and deep emotional connection.

Some women hit their stride right from the get-go. They are quick to accept the aspects of their husband and married life that they can't or shouldn't change. They're smart enough to take a measured view of the bigger picture, take a step back from unrealistic expectations, respect the words of their marriage vows, and take control of their own lives.

By following in the path of these happily married women, you will quickly see that you can attain fulfillment without giving up your hopes and dreams, without becoming someone you don't want to be. Sure, you may have to modify romance-novel expectations, but such actions can lead to a great sense of freedom. Yeah, you might have to praise your husband for a trivial action, but that gives him a finer appreciation of you.

And there may be times you take your husband to bed when you're not at the peak of your sex drive, but when you do that you are showing him how to be a more giving person himself.

As you apply the knowledge and practice the skills that you have gained from other happily married women, take the time to look at your life and the positive changes that you have the power to bring about. Remember that your husband is hard-wired and socialized to please you, and that you have the power to make him a better, nicer, more selfless, more giving man. As you know his nature, and start to work with, rather than against it, notice how your husband has become more respectful of you and is more likely to honor the differences between you. See how he begins to show an appreciation of your womanly perceptions, charms, and insights. See how all these positive consequences solidify your place at your husband's side.

When I wrote *The Secrets of Happily Married Men*, I noted the popular expression "When Mamma ain't happy, ain't nobody happy." The intent, of course, was to tell men about the importance of meeting their wives' needs. I continue to believe that the expression is totally true. Here, at the end of this book, I bring you the same sentiment, but in a broader sense.

Think about this version of the saying: "When Mamma's happy, everybody's happy." *You* have tremendous control over the level of happiness in your marriage and home. With this bookload of secrets, you can now take a leading role in having the kind of happy home life you've always wanted, with your family by your side, a husband who supports you, and kids who pick up on the positive energy that you bring to your home through your rich marriage.

Now that you know the secrets of happily married women—pass them on.

Notes

Chapter One

1. Blum, D. (1997). *Sex on the brain*. New York: Viking Press.
2. Sutherland, A. (2006, June 25). What Shamu taught me about a happy marriage. *The New York Times*. www.nytimes.com/2006/06/25/fashion/25love.html?ex=1151985600&en=feb4e>152a5c30208&ei=5070&emc=eta1.
3. Tannen, D. (2001). *You just don't understand*. New York: Quill.
4. Tannen, 2001.
5. Alter, J. (2007, April 9). How I live with cancer. *Newsweek*, pp. 30–37.
6. Gilbert, S. (2000). *A field guide to boys and girls*. New York: HarperCollins.
7. Moir, A., & Jessel, D. (1991). *Brain sex: The real difference between men and women*. New York: Delta.
8. Maccoby, D. (1998). *The two sexes*. Cambridge, MA: Harvard University Press, Belknap Press.
9. Beard, P. (1998, May). Dangerous minds. *Elle*.
10. Chen, L. H., Baker, S., Braver, E., & Guohua, L. (2000). Carrying passengers as a risk factor for crashes fatal to 16- and 17-year-old drivers. *Journal of the American Medical Association, 12*, 1580.
11. Badcock, C. (2000). *Evolutionary psychology*. Malden, MA: Blackwell.
12. Umberson D. (1987). Family status and health behavior: Social control as a dimension of social integration. *Journal of Health and Social Behavior, 28*, 316; Ross, C., Mirowsky, J., & Goldsteen, K. (1990). The impact of the family on health: Decade in review. *Journal of Marriage and the Family, 52*, 1058–1078.

Chapter Three

1. "The Top 5 Things Couples Argue About." (2007). Sixwise.com. http://www.sixwise.com/newsletters/06/02/22/the_top_5_things_couples_argue_about.htm.

2. Gottman, J., & Silver, N. (1999). *The seven principles for making marriage work.* New York: Crown.

3. Taylor, S. (2000). Biobehavioral responses to stress in females: Tend-and-befriend, not fight-or-flight. *Psychological Review, 107,* 411–429.

4. Love, P., & Stosny, S. (2007). *How to improve your marriage without talking about it: Finding love beyond words.* New York: Broadway Books.

5. Felson, R., & Cares, A. (2005, December). Gender and the seriousness of assaults on intimate partners and other victims. *Journal of Marriage and Family, 67,* 1182–1195.

6. Farrell, J. M. (2006, May 11). Romance, finance intertwined for today's newlyweds. *The Record,* Bergen County, New Jersey, p. B3.

7. Bugen, L. A., & Humenick, S. S. (1983). Instrumentality, expressiveness, and gender effects upon parent-infant interaction. *Basic and Applied Social Psychology, 4,* 239–251.

8. MacDonald, K. (Ed.). (1993). *Parent-child play: Descriptions and implications.* New York: State University of New York Press.

9. Moss, H. (1974). Early sex differences and mother-infant interaction. In R. C. Friedman, R. M. Richart, and R. L. van De Wiele (Eds.), *Sex differences in behavior* (pp. 149–163). Hoboken, NJ: Wiley.

10. Carlson, M. (2006, February). Family structure, father involvement, and adolescent behavioral outcomes. *Journal of Marriage and Family, 68,* 137–154.

11. Chesley, N. (2005, December). Blurring boundaries? Linking technology use, spillover, individual distress, and family satisfaction. *Journal of Marriage and Family, 67,* 1237–1248.

12. "Television trumps coition in bedrooms." (2006, January 30). The National Review of Medicine. http://www.nationalreviewofmedicine.com/news_in _brief/2006/nb3_issue02_jan30_pg2.html.

13. Gottman, J. (2005, June 25). *The math of marriage.* Paper presented at the ninth annual Smart Marriages Conference, Reno, Nevada.

14. Chethik, N. (2006). *VoiceMale.* New York: Simon & Schuster.

15. Gottman & Silver, 1999.

16. Gottman & Silver, 1999.

17. Gottman & Silver, 1999.

18. Stout, H. (2004, November 5). The key to a lasting marriage: Combat. *Wall Street Journal.* http://online.wsj.com/public/page.

19. Gottman & Silver, 1999.

20. Legato, M. (2005). *Why men never remember and women never forget.* Emmaus, PA: Rodale.

21. Schneider, F., Habel, U., Kessler, C., Salloum, J. B., & Posse, S. (2000). Gender differences in regional cerebral activity during sadness. *Human Brain Mapping, 9,* 226–238.

22. Legato, 2005.

23. Marano, H. E. (2003, July/August). The new sex scorecard. *Psychology Today*. http://psychologytoday.com/articles/pto-2832.html.

Chapter Four

1. Baron-Cohen, S. (2004). *The essential difference*. New York: Basic Books.
2. Baron-Cohen, 2004.
3. Marano, H. E. (2003, July/August). The new sex scorecard. *Psychology Today*. http://psychologytoday.com/articles/pto-2832.html.

Chapter Five

1. McCarthy, B. (1999). Marital style and its effects on sexual desire and functioning. *Journal of Family Psychotherapy, 10*(3), 1–11.
2. McCarthy, B., & McCarthy, E. (2003). *Rekindling desire*. New York: Brunner-Routledge.
3. Wilcox, A. J., Baird, D. D., Dunson, D. B., McConnaughey, D. R., Kesner, J. S., & Weinberg, C. R. (2004, July 19). On the frequency of intercourse around ovulation: Evidence for biological influences. *Human Reproduction, 19*, 1539–1543.
4. Brotherson, L. M. (2004). *And they were not ashamed*. Seattle: Elton-Wolf.
5. Mealey, L. (2000). *Sex differences: Developmental and evolutionary strategies*. San Diego: Academic Press.
6. Sileo, C. (1995, July). Studies put genetic twist on theories about sex and love. *Insight, 3*(10), 36–37.
7. Crenshaw, T. (1996). *The alchemy of love and lust*. New York: Putnam.
8. Maccoby, D. (1998). *The two sexes*. Cambridge, MA: Harvard University Press.
9. Basson, R. (2002). Women's sexual desire—disordered or misunderstood? *Journal of Sex and Marital Therapy, 28*(Suppl. 1), 17–28.

Chapter Six

1. Pew Research Center. (2006, February 13). *Are we happy yet?* http://pew research.org/social/pack.php?PackID=1.
2. Fisher, H. (2004). *Why we love: The nature and chemistry of romantic love*. New York: Owl Books.
3. Orbuch, T., House, J. S., Mero, R. P., & Webster, P. S. (1996, June). Marital quality over the life course. *Social Psychology Quarterly, 59*, 162–171.
4. Lucas, R. E., Clark, A. E., Georgellis, Y., & Diener, E. (2003). Reexamining adaptation and the set point model of happiness: Reactions to changes in marital status. *Journal of Personality and Social Psychology, 84*, 527–539.
5. Orbuch, House, Mero, & Webster, 1996.
6. Swanbrow, D. (2002, March 25). Study finds American men doing more housework. *The University Record*. University of Michigan. www.umich.edu/~urecord/0102/Mar25_02/16.htm.

7. Swanbrow, 2002.
8. Goodman, E. (2006, March 17). Redefining marital happiness. www.findarti cles.com/p/articles/mi_m1175/is_n9_v22/ai_6583416/print.
9. Online NewsHour. (1999, August 16). The first sex. www.pbs.org/news hour/gergen/july-dec99/fisher_8–16.html.
10. Wilcox, W., and Nock, S. (2006). What's love got to do with it? Equality, equity, commitment and woman's marital quality. *Social Forces*, 84(3), 1321–1345.
11. Bedell, G. (2006, June 11). What makes women happy? *Observer*. http://observer.guardian.co.uk/woman/story/0,,1792220,00.html.
12. Goodman, 2006.
13. Ohio working family survey shows women still do most housework. (1998). ScienceBlog. University of Cincinnati. www.scienceblog.com/community /older/1998/199802919.html.
14. Brinig, M. F., & Allen, D. W. (2000). These boots are made for walking: Why most divorce filers are women. *American Law Economic Review, 2*, 126–169; Ahrons, C. (1994). *The good divorce: Keeping your family together when your marriage comes apart.* New York: HarperCollins.
15. Braver, S. L., & O'Connell, D. (1998). *Divorced dads: Shattering the myths.* New York: Tarcher Putnam.
16. Gottman, J., & Silver, N. (1999). *The seven principles for making marriage work.* New York: Crown.
17. Goodman, 2006.

Chapter Seven
1. Bedell, G. (2006, June 11). What makes women happy? *Observer*. http://observer.guardian.co.uk/woman/story/0,,1792220,00.html.
2. Glass, S. (2002). *Not "just friends": Protect your relationship from infidelity and heal the trauma of betrayal.* New York: Free Press.
3. Babyak, M., Blumenthal, J. A., Herman, S., Khatri, P., Doraiswamy, M., Moore, K., Craighead, W. E., Baldewicz, T. T., & Krishnan, K. R. (2000). Exercise treatment for major depression: Maintenance of therapeutic benefit at 10 months. *Psychosomatic Medicine, 62*, 633–638.
4. Chethik, N. (2006). *VoiceMale*. New York: Simon & Schuster.
5. A psychology of satisfaction. (2005, October). *Harvard Women's Health Watch.* www.health.harvard.edu.
6. Bedell, 2006.
7. Bedell, 2006.
8. Kiesling, S., & Harris, G. T. (1989, October). The prayer war—Herbert Benson's research on health benefits of prayer. *Psychology Today*, pp. 65–66.

About the Authors

Scott Haltzman, M.D., is clinical assistant professor of psychiatry and human behavior at Brown University and medical director of NRI Community Services in Rhode Island. He is the author of *The Secrets of Happily Married Men*. He serves as a member of the "Love Network" for *Redbook*. His passion for saving marriages has led to appearances on the *Today Show*, *20/20*, *Good Morning America*, and features in *Time* magazine, the *New York Times*, and the *Washington Post*. You can reach him at DrScott@HappilyMarriedWomen.com.

Theresa Foy DiGeronimo, M.Ed., is the author of more than fifty books in the fields of parenting, education, and family relationships. She is the coauthor of *Raising Baby Green, College of the Overwhelmed,* and *Launching Our Black Children for Success,* all from Jossey-Bass. She is an adjunct professor of English at William Paterson University of New Jersey and also a high school teacher in her hometown of Hawthorne, New Jersey.